CAPITAL MARKET
and
Financial System in India

Asheesh Pandey

Assistant Professor of Finance,
Jaipuria Institute of Management, NOIDA

New Century Publications
New Delhi, India

NEW CENTURY PUBLICATIONS
4852 / 24, 1st Floor,
Ansari Road, Daryaganj,
New Delhi – 110 002 (India)

Tel.: 011-4101 7798; 4358 7398; 98112 66355
E-mail: info@newcenturypublications.com

www.newcenturypublications.com

Editorial office:
4800 / 24, Bharat Ram Road,
Ansari Road, Daryaganj,
New Delhi – 110 002

Edition: 2026

ISBN: **978-81-7708-365-1**

Published by New Century Publications and printed at Milan Enterprises, New Delhi.

Designs: Patch Creative Unit, New Delhi.

First Published: 2014

PRINTED IN INDIA

Dedicated to

My Parents

and

Neeta, Rohinesh, Kartikay

About the Book

The financial system of a country promotes savings by providing a wide variety of financial assets to the general public. Savings collected from the household sector are pooled together and allocated to various sectors of the economy for raising production levels. If the allocation of credit is judicious and socially equitable, it can help achieve the twin objectives of growth and social justice.

An understanding of financial markets—as part of the financial system—is important as they are at the core of the transmission mechanism of monetary policy. In India, financial markets have been developed with a specific emphasis on increasing allocative efficiency of resources and promoting financial stability. Financial markets in India comprise, in the main, money market, Government securities market, capital market, corporate debt market, credit market, and foreign exchange market.

Capital market plays a very important role in the development of financial system of any economy. It is a market where financial assets such as equities/debts are traded over a long period of time.

Although the capital market in India has a long history, it remained on the periphery of the financial system for a long time. Various reforms undertaken since the early 1990s by the Securities and Exchange Board of India (SEBI) and the Government have brought about a significant structural transformation in the Indian capital market. As a result, the Indian equity market has become modern and transparent.

The equity market has witnessed widespread development in infrastructure and its functioning is comparable to international standards. It has seen significant increase in growth and diversity in composition since early 1990s.

Author's Profile

Dr. Asheesh Pandey is currently Assistant Professor of Finance at Jaipuria Institute of Management, NOIDA. He is also the Programme Director for PGDM (Services) at the same Institute. He holds M.Com., MBA (Finance) and Ph.D. degrees from University of Delhi. With around 13 years of industry, research and teaching experience, he regularly contributes research papers in the area of finance to national and international journals including *Vision*, *Management of Labour Studies*, *AAMJAF* and *AJFA*.

Dr. Asheesh has also participated and presented papers in various national conferences and seminars. His research interest includes equity valuation, portfolio management, financial derivatives and corporate finance.

Contents

Preface

Financial System

The financial system of a country promotes savings by providing a wide variety of financial assets to the general public. Savings collected from the household sector are pooled together and allocated to various sectors of the economy for raising production levels. If the allocation of credit is judicious and socially equitable, it can help achieve the twin objectives of growth and social justice.

In the context of relatively underdeveloped capital market and with little internal resources, firms/economic entities depend largely on financial intermediaries for their fund requirements. A financial system performs the following functions, *inter alia*, for the smooth conduct of an economy:

1. It facilitates trading and hedging of risks. Risk mitigation reduces uncertainty and enables resources to flow towards most profitable projects. Such a situation raises the efficiency of investments and the rate of growth.
2. By acting as an efficient conduit for allocating resources, the financial system enables improvement in technical progress. Technological innovations take place when entrepreneurs exploit the best chances of successfully imitating technologies in their production processes and introducing new products.
3. To the extent that financial development leads to the creation of financial infrastructure and enables better and more efficient provision of goods and services, costs of transactions are lowered with positive spill over on development efforts.

Financial Markets

An understanding of financial markets—as part of financial system—is important as they are at the core of the transmission mechanism of monetary policy. In India, financial markets have been developed with a specific emphasis on increasing allocative efficiency of resources and promoting financial stability. Financial markets in India comprise, in the main, money market, Government securities market, capital market, corporate debt market, credit market, and foreign exchange market.

Till the early 1990s, most of the financial markets were characterised by controls over the pricing of financial assets, restrictions on flows or transactions, barriers to entry, low liquidity and high transaction costs. These characteristics came in the way of development of the markets and allocative efficiency of resources channelled through them. From 1991 onward, financial market reforms have emphasised the following: (a) easing restrictions on transactions, (b) reducing transaction costs, (c) introduction of new players/instruments, (d) free pricing of financial assets, (e) improvement in trading, clearing and settlement practices, (f) greater transparency, and (g) building of institutional infrastructure.

Integrated financial markets are a key element in the transmission process and hence for the smooth conduct of monetary policy. Financial integration also leads to a better diversification of risks and makes a positive contribution to financial stability by improving the capacity of economies to absorb shocks. On the other hand, fully integrated financial markets also pave the way for shocks to propagate more quickly among market participants, which could necessitate appropriate safeguards.

Financial markets in India have come a long way and are getting increasingly integrated domestically and globally. Reform measures in terms of free pricing, removal of barriers to flows and broad-based participation have yielded results in terms of fairly high degree of integration of the money market, the government securities market and the foreign exchange market, although in varying degrees. The money market and the foreign exchange market are reasonably well integrated, which is reflected in the high correlation coefficients between various money market rates and forward premia. The inter-linkage between the domestic money and international markets has also increased as is reflected in the increasing importance of interest rate differentials in the determination of forward premia. In general, the interest rate differential between the domestic money and international markets motivates market participants to shift funds between the markets.

Capital Market

Capital market plays a very important role in the development of financial system of any economy. It is a market where financial assets such as equities/debts are traded over a long period of time. It is an important source of raising long-term funds, both by government as well as by corporates. Capital market comprises of primary market and secondary market. Primary market is a market wherein companies raise new funds in the form of debt or equity and financial institutions invest in these securities. On the other hand, in secondary markets, securities once issued in primary market are traded among investors or traders on the recognized stock exchanges. Every country has a regulator of capital market which regulates the activities in such markets and also safeguards investors' interest. Securities Exchange Board of India (SEBI), set up in 1992, is the regulator for Indian capital market.

Capital market structure has evolved over time with the market practices and conditions generally reflecting the policies put in place. Till the onset of reforms in the early 1990s, raising of resources in the primary segment of the market was subject to several controls, disallowing pricing to be determined by market conditions. Trading in the secondary market was subject to opaque practices. The trading and settlement system was outdated and out of tune with internationally followed practices. The volumes, however, increased and securities continued to exist in physical form. Physical securities also created uncertainties for investors and increased the transaction costs. Besides, long and uncertain settlement cycles created serious problems for clearing houses. Informational flows to the market participants were also deficient. It was considered necessary to orient the SEBI to undertake the tasks of regulation and supervision. The SEBI was, for this purpose, given statutory powers through a separate legislation in 1992.

Although the capital market in India has a long history, during the most part, it remained on the periphery of the financial system. Various reforms undertaken since the early 1990s by the Securities and Exchange Board of India (SEBI) and the Government have brought about a significant structural transformation in the Indian capital market. As a result, the Indian equity market has become modern and transparent.

The equity market has witnessed wide-spread development in infrastructure and its functioning is comparable to international standards. It has seen significant increase in growth and diversity in composition since early 1990s.

Acknowledgements

I take this opportunity to place on record my deep sense of gratitude to Professor Sanjay Sehgal, Head, Department of Financial Studies, University of Delhi, for his constructive criticisms, invaluable suggestions and encouragement at every stage of the completion of this work. I also express my gratitude and thanks to the management of Jaipuria Institute of Management, NOIDA for allowing me time and providing all kinds of institutional support to accomplish this work.

I express my respect and thanks to my parents and grandmother for their blessings and moral support. Finally, I record my appreciation and affection for my wife Shrimati Neeta Pandey and my children Rohinesh and Kartikay.

New Delhi **Asheesh Pandey**

1

Indian Economy: An Overview

1.1 Human Resources

After China, India is the most populated country in the world with a headcount of 121 crore in 2011. Mainland China's population is 135 crore. India accounts for 17 percent of world population and having only 2.4 percent of total world area. India's population has increased rapidly since Independence in 1947. The population increased from 36.1 crore in 1951 to 43.9 crore in 1961, to 54.8 crore in 1971, and to 68.5 crore in 1981. The census of 1991 enumerated the population at 84.4 crore. 2001 census put India's population at 102.7 crore as on March 1, 2001.

The unabated growth of population is attributable to a sharp decline in death-rate coupled with relatively high birth-rate. The 2001 Census recorded birth-rate and death-rate at 25.8 and 8.5 percent respectively for the year 2001. During 1951-71, birth-rate remained almost unchanged while death-rate declined appreciably. The death-rate has fallen due to improved health conditions, control of epidemics, better handling of famine conditions, and general improvement in the standard of living. There has been a significant decline in the infant mortality rate since Independence.

However, birth-rate in India is still very high, hovering in the vicinity of 26 per thousand. Many social and economic factors are responsible for high birth-rate. These include universality of marriage, preference for male children, illiteracy, and poverty. The rapid growth of population has seriously hampered developmental efforts.

The alarming growth of India's population calls for a systematic and effective population policy to curb the undesirable trend. The post-Independence population explosion has nullified, to a large extent, the gains of developmental efforts.

The policy of the Government of India to control population has relied excessively on family planning programme. Ever since the launching of the First Five Year Plan (1951-56), family planning has occupied an important place in the development strategy of the Government. Successive plans have allocated more and more resources for the implementation of family planning schemes. In 1966, a separate Department of Family Planning was created in the Union Ministry of Health. However, the results have not been encouraging.

The National Population Policy (NPP) 2000 outlined the long-term objective of attaining a stable population by 2045, a level consistent with the requirements of sustainable economic growth, social development and environment protection. Apart from implementation of the National Population Policy involving all social sector programmes, the State Governments too will have to play an important role in improving the social, economic and demographic indicators especially in the high fertility regions. In the long-run, it is necessary to have an explicit demographic vision of attaining less than half percent annual growth rate of population by the end of next decade. This would involve significant upgradation of the status of women in the society and attainment of almost 100 percent literacy among adult females.

1.2 Economic Planning

India began the process of planned economic development with the start of the First Five Year Plan in April 1951. The main objective of planning was identified as that of initiating a process of development which would raise living standards and open out to the people new opportunities for a richer and more varied life. The manner in which this objective has been translated into specific objectives has varied from Plan to Plan.

However, in a broad sense, the basic objectives of

planning in India can be grouped under four heads: (a) growth, (b) modernisation, (c) self-reliance, and (d) social justice. In one form or another, these objectives, albeit with varying emphasis, reflect the views of all sections of the population and represent a national consensus on the aims of planning.

Since 1951, India has completed eleven Five Year Plans and the implementation of the Twelfth Five Year Plan (2012-17) is underway. Each Plan takes into account the experience of the previous Plan and attempts to make the necessary directional changes and emphasis. In fact, the beginning and the end of a Plan are important dates in the economic history of India. Each Plan is both an assessment of the past and a call for the future.

At the time of the launching of First Five Year Plan (1951-56), India was faced with three formidable problems, viz. severe food shortage, mounting inflation and the influx of refugees in the wake of partition of the country in 1947. The First Plan had to address these problems on an urgent basis.

The Second Five Year Plan (1956-61) was formulated and implemented in an atmosphere of economic stability. Agricultural targets fixed in the First Plan had been achieved and inflation had registered a fall. The time was ripe to shift focus from agriculture to industry to give a big boost to the economy on modern lines. Hence, the Second Plan concentrated on the development of heavy and basic industries to lay the foundations for future industrialisation of the Indian economy. The following industries received special emphasis: iron and steel, chemicals, fertilisers, heavy engineering and machine building industry. It is also noteworthy that in 1956, Government announced its Industrial Policy (called by some as the economic constitution of India) which accepted the establishment of a socialistic pattern of society as the goal of economic policy.

The experience of the first two Plans had shown that agriculture was the backbone of the economy. Accordingly, the Third Five Year Plan (1961-66) gave top priority to agriculture but it also laid adequate emphasis on the development of basic industries which were vital for rapid development of the economy. In fact, the Third Plan set as its goal the establishment of a self-reliant and self-generating economy.

Planned development efforts were disrupted when the country came under severe shocks such as hostilities with Pakistan (1965), droughts for two successive years (1965-66 and 1966-67), devaluation of the rupee (1966) and inflationary pressure. On account of these adverse circumstances, the draft outline of the Fourth Plan prepared in 1966 had to be abandoned. Instead, three Annual Plans (1966-67, 1967-68 and 1968-69) were prepared and implemented.

The planning process was resumed when the Fourth Five Year Plan (1969-74) became operational in 1969. It set before itself two main objectives: (a) growth with stability, and (b) progressive achievement of self-reliance.

The Fifth Five Year Plan (1974-79) was introduced when the country was reeling under severe economic strains such as run-away inflation caused by unprecedented increase in international oil prices in the wake of 1973 Gulf Crisis and the failure of the Government to takeover the wholesale trade in wheat. The Plan could not complete its five years because it was terminated at the end of the fourth year (i.e. in March 1978) by the new Janata Party Government at the Centre.

The political turmoil of the late 1970s witnessed two Sixth Plans—(a) The Sixth Five Year Plan (1978-83) of the Janata Party Government which was abandoned with the change of Government at the Centre in 1980 and (b) The Sixth Five Year Plan (1980-85) introduced by the new Government led by Mrs. Indira Gandhi. The latter ran its full course successfully. It focused on direct attack on poverty.

The Seventh Five Year Plan (1985-90) sought to emphasise policies and programmes to increase foodgrains production, employment opportunities and productivity.

Eighth Five Year Plan which was to begin in April 1990

covering the period 1990-95 could not be finalised on time and hence there was a plan gap of two years. It took off in April 1992 covering the period 1992-97. This was followed by the Ninth Five Year Plan (1997-2002). The Tenth Five Year Plan (2002-07) was completed on March 31, 2007. In June 2005, the Government released the Mid-Term Appraisal of the Tenth Plan. The Eleventh Five Year Plan (2007-12) started on April 1, 2007 and ended on March 31, 2012. The Twelfth Five Year Plan (2012-17) is underway.

1.3 Agriculture and Rural Development

At the time of Independence in 1947, Indian agriculture was traditional and stagnant in every respect. It was characterised by feudal land relations, primitive technology, and the resultant low productivity per hectare. The first task of Indian Government in the immediate post-Independence period was, therefore, to initiate growth process in agriculture on modern lines. Modernisation of agriculture was required both in terms of technological and institutional changes. Abolition of intermediaries in agriculture, like *zamindars* and *jagirdars*, was accomplished soon after Independence.

The process of planned economic development in India began with the launching of First Five Year Plan in April 1951. At that time, the country was faced with severe food shortage and mounting inflation. The Plan accorded pride of place to programmes for agriculture and community development. This was a natural priority for the Plan which sought to raise the standard of living in rural areas and cope with food shortages.

In the mid-1960s, a new technology in the form of high-yielding varieties (HYVs) was introduced for cereals. Apart from the new technology, public investment in agriculture, particularly in irrigation, was stepped up significantly. The public sector played an important role in promoting agricultural research and education. Large investments were made for the development of research system under the aegis of the Indian Council of Agricultural Research (ICAR) and the State Agricultural Universities. Simultaneously, a well-designed extension network was created for disseminating new technologies to the farmers. Successive Five Year Plans have aimed at improving irrigation facilities, encouraging the use of fertilisers, improved varieties of seeds, implements and machinery and institutional credit. As a result, there has been a significant increase in the use of modern inputs leading to higher productivity and production. Satisfactory progress has been made not only in the production of major foodgrains but also in horticultural crops.

Another change of consequence was the introduction of a system of support prices, procurement and public distribution of major items of agricultural produce. Several changes have taken place in agricultural credit and marketing. The system of cooperative credit has spread, lessening the dependence of the cultivators on the exploitative practices of the village moneylenders. In agricultural marketing, the dominant role of the Food Corporation of India and the growth of marketing and processing cooperatives has helped both farmers and consumers. These and other changes in the field of credit and marketing have altered the very unequal relationship between the farmer and the trader.

Although agriculture is still the backbone of the Indian economy, at least in terms of employment, the impulses of reforms have been relatively less in scope and depth in this sector. It is noteworthy that reforms in agricultural sector were introduced only towards the end of the 1990s. Nevertheless, a series of policy initiatives have been undertaken in this sector as well. These include: (a) partial decontrol of fertiliser prices, (b) removal of bottlenecks in agricultural marketing, (c) relaxation of restrictions under the Essential Commodities Act, 1955, (d) introduction of forward trading in important commercial crops, (e) replacement of the Revamped Public Distribution System with Targeted Public Distribution System, (f) establishment of Rural Infrastructural Development Fund, and, (g) replacement of quantitative controls by tariff.

Still further, micro credit, routed through self-help groups (SHGs), has emerged as a visible credit channel to the poor as their access to conventional credit channels is constrained by the requirement of collateral and high transaction cost. The National Horticulture Mission was launched on April 1, 2005. The Mission will ensure end-to-end approach having backward and forward linkages covering research, production, post-harvest management, processing and marketing.

In the 2005-06 Union Budget, the Government proposed to introduce a new scheme called Development of Agricultural Marketing Infrastructure, Grading and Standardisation and a sum of ₹ 72 crore was allocated for the purpose. The objective of this scheme is to induce large investments from the private and cooperative sectors for setting up agriculture markets, marketing infrastructure and support services such as grading, standardization and quality certification. Assistance will be available in the form of credit-linked, back-ended subsidy and will be implemented through National Bank for Agriculture and Rural Development (NABARD) and the National Co-operative Development Corporation (NCDC).

The current deceleration in agriculture is the root cause of the problem of rural distress that has surfaced in many parts of the country and reached crisis levels in some. The strategy to raise agricultural output should comprise the following elements: (a) improve water management, rain water harvesting and watershed development, (b) reclaim degraded land and focus on soil quality, (c) bridge the knowledge gap through effective extension, (d) diversify into high value outputs, fruits, vegetables, flowers, herbs and spices, medicinal plants, bamboo, bio-diesel etc., but with adequate measures to ensure food security, (e) promote animal husbandry and fishery, (f) provide easy access to credit at affordable rates, (g) improve the incentive structure and functioning of markets, and (h) refocus on land reforms issues.

1.4 Industry and Infrastructure

The post-Independence industrial development of India has taken place within the framework of economic planning. The First Five Year Plan (1951-56) did not pay due attention to the industrial sector because it was mainly concerned with the removal of imbalances in the agricultural sector created by the partition of India in 1947. The Second Five Year Plan (1956-61) was basically a plan for the establishment of heavy and key industries. The successive plans have laid varying emphasis on the industrial development of the country.

Industrial sector of the Indian economy developed fairly rapidly during the first fifteen years (1951-66) of planned economic development. After that the pace of industrialisation slowed down, particularly in the capital goods sector. This so-called industrial retrogression was explained in terms of a host of factors, the chief among them being:

1. Exogenous causes like Chinese aggression (1962), Indo-Pak conflict (1965), and Bangladesh Crisis (1971).
2. Successive droughts of 1965-66 and 1966-67 and again in 1971-72 which disrupted the supply of raw materials and the demand for industrial goods emanating from the rural sector.
3. Oil crisis of 1973 resulting in cost-push inflation.

Some economists believe that the rigid industrial licensing policies and other controls coupled with bureaucratic hurdles also hampered the growth of the industrial sector after the mid-1960s.

Responding to the macroeconomic crisis of late 1980s, a programme of liberalisation, privatisation, and globalisation was initiated in July 1991 when the Government announced its new industrial policy in the Parliament. It removed industrial licensing, reduced the number of industries reserved for the public sector, abolished restrictions on investment and expansion under the Monopolies and Restrictive Trade Practices (MRTP) Act, 1969, allowed automatic approval of foreign investment, eliminated quantitative import restrictions on intermediate and capital goods. No doubt, the reform measures have created a favourable environment for industry to upgrade its technology and build-up capacity in order to cater to growing domestic and external demand.

Following the reform measures, there was an initial spurt in industrial activities. However, it was short-lived and deceleration set in from 1996-97. The industrial deceleration was due to a number of structural and cyclical factors such as normal business and investment cycles, a lack of both domestic and external demand, continuing high real interest rates, infrastructure bottlenecks in power and transport, and lack of reforms in land and labour markets.

The process of industrial liberalisation started in 1991 is continuing. Private sector has been invited to invest in oil exploration and refining. Similarly, power sector is now open to both domestic and foreign private investment. Government has also allowed private sector activities in the mining industry. Industrial liberalisation after 1991 has proved a boon for the Indian economy, though there are some grey areas.

In another significant move, the Government enacted the Micro, Small and Medium Enterprises Development (MSMED) Act, 2006. This legislation for facilitating promotion and development and enhancing the competitiveness of micro, small and medium enterprises became operational from October 2, 2006.

By and large, Indian industry has upgraded technology and product quality to a significant degree and met the challenge of openness after being protected for so long. The Competition Act, 2002 passed by the Parliament seeks to establish a pro-competitive legal framework, contain anti-competitive practices and abuses of dominance and yield better regulation of markets.

Industrial progress of India over the last 60 years since Independence has been quite satisfactory. The country has achieved near self-sufficiency in the production of manufactured goods as reflected in the composition of imports which mainly consist of petroleum products, chemicals, and capital goods. Industrial progress has also led to the growth of technological and managerial skills, and industrial and scientific research. The process of economic reforms in India seems irreversible. There is enough evidence that Government is withdrawing, though gradually, as a controller and licenser of private activity and allowing competition and market forces to guide investment decisions.

Availability of adequate, efficient and affordable infrastructural facilities constitutes the core of development strategy and efforts. Economic infrastructure, covering, *inter alia*, power, transportation, and communications, creates congenial conditions for growth process through its backward and forward linkages. The demand for infrastructural services has increased rapidly after industrial liberalisation of the Indian economy. Unfortunately, infrastructural bottlenecks remain the biggest stumbling block of industrial progress in the country. By their very nature, infrastructure projects involve huge initial investments, long gestation periods and high risk.

India's industrial policy soon after Independence in 1947 was shaped broadly in terms of the Industrial Policy Resolution of 1948. That Resolution emphasised clearly the responsibility of the Government in promoting, assisting and regulating the development of industry in the national interest. It envisaged for the public sector an increasingly active role. This role was to be particularly significant in the establishment and development of heavy and basic industries. Certain crucial sectors for industrial development were reserved for Government initiative.

The 1948 Resolution was reviewed in the light of experience gained, and the new Industrial Policy Resolution was placed before Parliament by the Prime Minister on April 30, 1956. As the Resolution put it, "The adoption of the socialist pattern of society as the national objective, as well as the need for planned and rapid development, require that all

industries of basic and strategic importance, or in the nature of public utility services, should be in the public sector. Other industries which are essential and require investment on a scale which only the State, in present circumstances, could provide, have also to be in the public sector. The state has, therefore, to assume direct responsibility for the future development of industries over a wider area."

Started with great fanfare after Independence, public enterprises got afflicted with various ills over the years. Public sector was assigned the job of providing infrastructural facilities from the very beginning. However, its performance has been unsatisfactory. It is abundantly clear from chronic power shortages in different parts of the country which adversely affect industrial and agricultural output. Similarly, shortage of railway wagons, bad roads, congestion at sea ports and inefficient telecommunication system have seriously hampered the growth of private industry and trade. These infrastructural bottlenecks continue till this day. Government is now soliciting the participation of private sector to augment and improve infrastructural facilities in the economy.

The unsatisfactory performance of the public sector in providing adequate infrastructural facilities is mainly attributed to the following factors: (a) lack of technological upgradation, (b) inadequate attention to research and development, (c) delays in completion and consequent increase in costs of public projects, (d) over-staffing, (e) labour indiscipline, (f) under-utilisation of installed capacity, (g) excessive political interference, (h) bureaucratic instead of professionalised management, and (i) undue emphasis on capital-intensive technology. Infrastructure development is an integral part of the economic reforms programme started in India in the early 1990s.

Policy makers have worked on problems of infrastructure policy for over a decade. There has been substantial progress in some areas. The broad outlines now appear to be falling into place. The key principles seem to involve new institutional arrangements, well-enforced user charges, exploiting new technologies, private sector participation and a regulatory framework that promotes competition.

1.5 Fiscal Policy

Fiscal policy is an important instrument of the general economic policy of a government. It is concerned with the use of a government's taxation and expenditure powers to influence economic activities in an economy at the aggregate level. It also deals with financial relations between different tiers of government in a federal polity. Through the medium of budget, it determines government expenditure, borrowing requirements and issue of new currency. It also determines private spending through taxation measures.

It may be recalled that the external payments crisis of 1991, which led to the initiation of economic reforms in India, was the result of deteriorating fiscal situation during the latter half of 1980s. This period was marked by high and persistent fiscal deficits, accompanied by large revenue deficits. This had led to a significant enlargement of Government borrowings from financial intermediaries and increased financing of Government deficit through automatic monetisation which aggravated price rise. When the Indian economy faced an unprecedented macroeconomic crisis in 1991, fiscal consolidation constituted a major objective of the policy response. This consolidation was to be achieved through reduction in the size of budget deficit and public debt in relation to GDP. For this purpose, it became necessary to: (a) enhance tax and non-tax revenue, (b) curtail current expenditure growth, (c) restructure public sector undertaking, including disinvestment, (d) improve fiscal-monetary co-ordination, and (e) deregulate financial system.

Apart from these reforms aimed at fiscal consolidation, a number of institutional measures were also taken during the 1990s. Public sector restructuring and disinvestments were undertaken with a view to increase the efficiency of the public sector undertakings and also to provide additional resources to the Government. The need for improvements in budgetary practices led to the enactment of the Fiscal Responsibility and Budget Management (FRBM) Act, 2003 which ushered the Indian economy in an era of fiscal consolidation based on fiscal policy rules.

The financing of fiscal deficit is another area, which underwent significant changes in the post-reform period. With the discontinuation of *ad hoc* 91-day Treasury Bills in April 1997, automatic monetisation of deficits was eliminated. Greater reliance on borrowing at market-related interest rates has led to a substantial lowering of statutory pre-emption of institutional resources for the Government. This has also facilitated development of the market for Government securities which has witnessed remarkable changes in the last few years.

1.6 Money, Credit and Prices

Monetary policy refers to the expansion or contraction of money and credit supply in an economy. Since monetary policy includes the regulation of both the volume and allocation of credit therefore credit policy is a part of the overall monetary policy. Monetary policy operates through changes in the stock of money and changes in the cost and availability of credit. The operation of monetary policy rests on the interrelationship between the stock of money, output and prices. Through money creation, credit is made available to productive enterprises. The availability of credit has favourable impact on output. Simultaneously, increase in money supply raises demand, exerting pressure on prices. The output effect and the price effect must be considered together to assess the overall effect of a monetary measure on the economy.

In tune with the national economic objectives, RBI has followed a monetary policy usually called the policy of *controlled expansion*. The money supply has expanded sufficiently to meet the growing needs of industry and trade.

However, it has been ensured that the expansion is not reckless. Broadly speaking, the expansion of money supply has been somewhat more than the increase in output thereby allowing a reasonable increase in the price level.

Budgetary deficits of the Central Government are an important cause for monetary expansion in India. In fact, monetary policy has played a subservient role to fiscal policy in India. Therefore, the main emphasis of the RBI has been on controlling secondary expansion of money, i.e. credit given by commercial banks to other sectors of the economy. While restraining the banking system in this regard, the RBI has ensured that the credit needs of priority sectors (agriculture, small-scale industries) are adequately met.

The RBI has pursued its monetary policy through a variety of instruments at its command. These include: bank rate policy, open market operations, variable reserve ratio and selective credit controls (now abolished). The twin objectives of monetary policy, viz. maintaining price stability and ensuring availability of adequate credit to productive sectors of the economy to support growth have remained unchanged, though their relative emphasis has varied depending on the circumstances. In line with this, in recent years, a preference emerged for a soft and flexible interest rate environment within the framework of macroeconomic stability. At the same time, the large inflows of external capital have contributed to the liquidity conditions remaining very comfortable. Consequently, the emphasis of monetary policy within the broad objectives of price stability and growth has been on liquidity management so as to ensure orderly conditions in financial markets without impeding the legitimate credit needs of industry.

The Reserve Bank of India (RBI) has largely been successful in bringing the organised sector of the money market well under its control. RBI is also playing a more active role in the provision of rural finance and is devoting special attention to the problem of promoting banking development in parts of the country in which it has hitherto been lacking. These developments have strengthened the credit system materially. RBI has wide powers for regulation and supervision of the credit policy of banks. More than these legal powers, it is the moral prestige of the RBI and the close understanding between its management and the management of public sector and private sector banks that is of special importance in the alignment of the banking system to the needs of a planned economy.

Price stability is of prime concern for a developing country like India. The term price stability is not used here in a rigid sense to mean price fixity. A modest increase of 2-3 percent in price level per annum is compatible, sometimes even desirable, with the general connotation of price stability. Since price rise is closely linked with the supply of money therefore monetary policy holds the key to price stability. This is why the economists stress growth with stability as the ideal objective of economic policy of a country.

Price stability is desired in the Indian context because majority of the population belongs to unorganised sector without protection against the onslaughts of inflation. Price stability is a pre-requisite for a successful development strategy, particularly in the context of the implementation of Five Year Plans. Domestic price stability is required also to boost exports.

Judicious demand and supply management policies are required to counteract inflationary tendencies. In spite of strong inflationary pressures in the world economy, India has successfully prevented inflation from getting out of hand. Government has focused attention on the price stability of certain essential commodities. This has been ensured by maintaining demand and supply balance at commodity level.

In short, following are the important elements of the price policy of the Government of India: (a) Some basic commodities like foodgrains and sugar are made available to consumers at fixed prices through a vast network of fair price shops. (b) Buffer stock operations are undertaken to maintain open market prices of certain essential goods with reasonable range. (c) Imports of essential goods (e.g. vegetable oils and sugar) are allowed when necessary and exports held back to ensure adequate supplies of essential commodities (e.g. tea).

1.7 Financial Institutions and Financial Markets

Financial sector of an economy is a multi-faceted term. It refers to the whole gamut of legal and institutional arrangements, financial intermediaries, markets, and instruments with both domestic and external dimensions.

Finance is the life blood of a modern economy. A financial system helps to mobilise the financial surpluses of an economy and transfer them to areas of financial deficit. It is the linchpin of any development strategy. The financial system promotes savings by providing a wide variety of financial assets to the general public. Savings collected from the household sector are pooled together and allocated to various sectors of the economy for raising production levels. If the allocation of credit is judicious and socially equitable, it can help achieve the twin objectives of growth and social justice.

India has a long and chequered history of financial intermediation, particularly commercial banking. At the beginning of the 20th century, India had insurance companies (both life and general) and a functional stock exchange. Even before the setting up of the Reserve Bank of India in 1935, the country had market for money, Government securities and foreign exchange. The financial system was, however, characterised by paucity of funds and instruments, limited number of players and lack of depth and openness. It was primarily a bank-based system.

Soon after Independence in 1947, Government of India followed a policy of social control of important financial institutions. This was reflected in the nationalisation of the Reserve Bank of India (RBI) in 1948, takeover of the then Imperial Bank of India (rechristened as State Bank of India) in

1956, nationalisation of life insurance business and the creation of Life Insurance Corporation of India (LIC) also in 1956, nationalisation of 14 major commercial banks in 1969, nationalisation of general insurance companies and the setting up of General Insurance Corporation (GIC) in 1972, and nationalisation of 6 more commercial banks in 1980.

As a result of state domination, India's financial system was characterised by barriers to entry, control over pricing of financial assets, high transaction costs and restrictions on movement of funds from one market segment to another. It was in this backdrop that wide-ranging financial sector reforms were introduced as an integral part of the economic reforms programme started in early 1990s. These reforms have paved the way for integration among various segments of the financial system. It is widely accepted that reduction/removal of financial repression has enhanced the efficiency and potential growth of the Indian economy.

1.8 Employment and Labour Welfare

In the early 1990s, the process of economic reforms was set in motion when the Government introduced a series of measures to reduce control on industries, particularly large industries. The workers have opposed economic liberalisation policy for fear of unemployment while entrepreneurs have welcomed it in the hope of new opportunities to improve Indian industries. The new economic policy has directly affected industrial relations in the country, because the Government has to play a dual role, one of protecting the interest of the workers, and second to allow a free interplay of the market forces. The two roles can be conflicting, and the Government needs to make relevant changes in the labour legislations to balance the position. As a result of the new economic policy, there is increased competition in the market which Indian industries are finding difficult to face due to old technology, and legislations which do not allow for closures, retrenchments, layoffs etc. The management is, therefore, demanding major changes in labour legislations.

Likewise, the structural changes have left trade unions bewildered. They are looking for new forms of struggle to channelise the growing discontent and anger of the working class. Due to the various structural changes taking place, the role of the trade unions is also undergoing a change. Till now the unions had basically been bargaining for security of jobs, wages, working conditions etc. In the changed scenario, they have to redefine their role and objectives, and come up with new ways of facing the management. They have now to give more importance to education, training, retraining and counselling of the workers.

The Government is trying to transform the economy into a vibrant, outward looking, liberalised market economy driven by the forces of competition, productivity and efficiency. It expects the employers and the workers to appreciate the inevitability of change and to maximise the benefits to be derived from the new work ethos. The Government of India set up the Second National Commission on Labour (Chairman: Ravindra Verma) in October 1999. The Commission was asked to review the post-globalisation scenario and suggest rationalisation of the labour laws.

The Commission submitted its report to the Prime Minister on June 29, 2002. The Commission, in its report, has given the Government a go ahead for controversial labour reforms. It has favoured the proposed amendments in the Industrial Disputes Act which will make closure of firms and workers' lay-offs much easier. It found nothing objectionable in amending the Contract Law to employ workers on contract even if the jobs are permanent. The Commission also stressed the need for an expanded social security network in the country to take care of workers' interests.

Labour reforms in India, in the context of globalisation, are much desired, but also feared and misinterpreted. The issue has been a touchy one ever since the liberalisation era began under the Narsimha Rao government in the early 1990s.

Economic reforms, by removing barriers to entry, have created competitive markets. Fiscal stabilisation has resulted in drastic reduction in budgetary support to the public sector commercial enterprises while exposing these enterprises to increased competition from private sector. A shift from long protected non-competitive to increasingly competitive markets since 1991 has reduced wasteful utilisation of both capital and labour. Side by side, increasing competitive pressures have also involved a shift from high-margin-low-volume environment of the earlier period to the high-volume-low-margin situation. This is expected to induct greater labour force in the production process.

It may be recalled that the National Democratic Alliance (NDA) Government had also proposed certain labour reforms but could not muster the courage to carry them out. For example, the Finance Minister in his 2001-2002 budget speech had proposed amendment of Section 10 of the Contract Labour Act, (a) to facilitate outsourcing of activities without any restrictions, and (b) to offer contract appointments. In the same budget speech, he proposed changes in the Industrial Disputes Act. According to Chapter VB of the Industrial Disputes Act, employers in specified industrial establishments must obtain prior approval of the appropriate government authority for effecting lay-offs, retrenchment and closure, after following the prescribed procedure. The Finance Minister proposed that these provisions of the Act be applied to industrial establishments employing not less than 1,000 workers instead of 100 workers as at present. However, implementing these reforms would require much imagination and political will.

1.9 Environmental Concerns

Natural and environmental resources are the basis of all economic activities. Soil, forests, mines, water, air and other natural resources are productive assets of an economy. In fact, productivity of an economic system depends to a large extent on the supply and quality of its natural resources. Poor quality of water and air adversely affects the health of population, causing reduced labour productivity and premature mortality. Similarly, soil degradation and erosion leads to reduced and inferior quality agricultural output.

India embarked on a programme of planned economic development with the launching of First Five Year Plan in 1951. Ever since, the emphasis has been on removal of poverty and unemployment and all possible instruments of economic policy have been used to achieve the twin-objectives. However, the euphoria for rapid economic development created enormous pressure on country's natural resources. Forests were subjected to rapid degradation due to growing demand for forest-based inputs for industrial use. Other natural resources, namely water, land, and air became dumping grounds for industrial wastes, often with toxic materials. In short, environmental issues were completely overlooked during the first two decades (1950-70) of economic development.

It was in the early 1970s that Government realised the need for environmental protection as an integral part of industrial policy. Unfortunately, considerable damage had already been done to India's natural resources by the time preventive measures were taken. Thus, land/soil degradation has taken place due to floods, water-logging, salinity, indiscriminate mining and faulty agricultural practices. Similarly, forest wealth is dwindling due to withdrawal of forest products (timber, fuel wood), overgrazing, forest fires and location of development projects in forest areas.

1.10 Foreign Trade

Over the last 60 years, India's foreign trade has undergone a complete change in terms of composition and direction. The exports cover a wide range of traditional and non-traditional items while imports mainly consist of capital goods, petroleum products, raw materials, and chemicals to meet the ever-increasing needs of a developing and diversifying economy.

For about 40 years (1950-90), foreign trade of India suffered from strict bureaucratic and discretionary controls. Similarly, foreign exchange transactions were tightly controlled by the Government and the Reserve Bank of India. From Independence in 1947 till mid-1990s, India, with some exceptions, always faced deficit in its balance of payments, i.e. imports always exceeded exports. This was characteristic of a developing country struggling for reconstruction and modernisation of its economy. Imports galloped because of increasing requirements of capital goods, defence equipment, petroleum products, and raw materials. Exports remained relatively sluggish owing to lack of exportable surplus, competition in the international market, inflation at home, and increasing protectionist policies of the developed countries.

Beginning mid-1991, the Government of India introduced a series of reforms to liberalise and globalise the Indian economy. Reforms in the external sector of India were intended to integrate the Indian economy with the world economy. Reform of trade and exchange rate policy was a critical element in structural reform and a great deal was done in this area. The exchange rate adjustments in July 1991 and the trade policy announced subsequently, considerably reduced the reliance upon licensing control of imports and created a more favourable exchange rate for exports.

Since the initiation of economic reforms, India's outward orientation has increased considerably. The destination pattern of Indian exports has remarkably changed in the sense that the importance of developing countries as an export market has considerably increased. There are, however, concerns that the country has not been able to fully utilise its potential in international trade. In contrast to the dramatic changes in exports of East Asia, India's experience has seemingly fallen short of expectation. India's share in global trade did not rise as impressively and the commodity structure of India's exports remained almost unchanged until the mid-1990s.

The major trade policy changes in the post-1991 period

included simplification of procedures, removal of quantitative restrictions, and substantial reduction in the tariff rates. A significant development in the current account of balance of payments in the 1990s was the remarkable growth in the export of invisibles to the rest of the world. This was made possible by growth in information and communication related services like computer software, hardware, internet, e-commerce and telecommunication sector.

India's approach to openness has been cautious, contingent on achieving certain preconditions to ensure an orderly process of liberalisation and ensuring macroeconomic stability. This approach has been vindicated in recent years with the growing incidence of financial crises elsewhere in the world. All the same, the policy regime in India in regard to liberalisation of the foreign sector has witnessed very significant change.

To conclude, for almost three decades after Independence in 1947, development pattern of India was characterised by strong centralised planning, government ownership of basic and key industries, excessive regulation and control of private enterprise, trade protectionism through tariff and non-tariff barriers and a cautious and selective approach towards foreign capital. This so-called inward-looking, import substitution strategy of economic development began to be widely questioned with the beginning of 1980s. Policy makers started realising the drawbacks of this strategy which inhibited competitiveness and efficiency and produced a much lower rate of growth than expected.

Consequently, economic reforms were set in motion, though on a modest scale, when controls on industries were reduced by the 1985 Industrial Policy. The economic reforms programme got a big boost when the Government announced a New Industrial Policy in the Indian Parliament on July 24, 1991. Since then, it is liberalisation, privatisation and globalisation all the way and the process is underway. In the new liberalised industrial and trade environment, the Government is progressively assuming the role of a promoter, facilitator and catalytic agent instead of a regulator and controller of economic activities.

India is now Asia's third largest economy and has the world's fourth largest foreign exchange reserves. Technology, competition, and benchmarking to the best international practices are the driving forces of India's development efforts. The country is making rapid strides in all these areas. Technology is getting upgraded rapidly and competition in the market place has become fierce. The vibrant information technology (IT) industry is contributing immensely by providing information about latest technology and international business practices.

It can safely be said that India is no longer a country of scarcities and shortages. Foodgrain stocks are plentiful, foreign exchange reserves are overflowing, inflation rate is moderate and under control, exports are buoyant, exchange rate is flexible and the country is well integrated with the world economy. All these features of new India are amply reflected in a relatively high rate of economic growth and a significant reduction in poverty ratio over the last two decades. India's gradual and cautious approach to economic reforms has proved well-founded and the country is placed on a firm footing for future forays into domestic and global economic activities.

2

Financial Sector of India: Pre-Reforms Period

At the time of Independence in 1947, India had a fairly well-developed banking system. The process of financial development in independent India has hinged effectively on the development of commercial banking, with impetus given to industrialisation based on the initiatives provided in the five year plans.

2.1 State Control of Financial Sector

Soon after Independence in 1947, Government of India followed a policy of social control of important financial institutions. The nationalisation of the Reserve Bank of India (RBI) in 1948 marked the beginning of this policy. This was followed by the takeover of the then Imperial Bank of India in 1955 which was rechristened as State Bank of India. In 1956, 245 life insurance companies were nationalised and merged into the newly created Life Insurance Corporation of India (LIC). In another significant development, Government nationalised 14 major commercial banks in 1969. The year 1972 saw the nationalisation of general insurance companies and the setting up of General Insurance Corporation (GIC). In 1980, 6 more commercial banks were nationalized and brought under public ownership.

Trade and industrial activities during the 1950s, and the 1960s reflected the dominance of banking as the critical source. The number of banks and branches had gone up, notwithstanding the consolidation of small banks, and the support given to the community-operative credit movement. Functionally, banks catered to the needs of the organised industrial and trading sectors. The primary sector consisting of agriculture, forestry, and fishing had to depend largely on their own financing and on sources outside the commercial banks.

The course of development of financial institutions and markets during the post-Independence period has been largely guided by the process of planned development pursued in India with emphasis on mobilisation of savings and channelising investment to meet Plan priorities. The adoption of bank-dominated financial development strategy was aimed at meeting the sectoral credit needs, particularly of agriculture and industry. Towards this end, the RBI (nationalised in 1948) concentrated on regulating and developing mechanisms for institution building.

The commercial banking network was expanded to cater to the requirements of general banking and for meeting the short-term working capital requirements of industry and agriculture. Specialised development finance institutions (DFIs) with majority ownership of the RBI were set up to meet the long-term financing requirements of industry and agriculture. To facilitate the growth of these institutions, a mechanism to provide concessional finance to these institutions was also put in place by the RBI.

2.2 Nationalisation of Imperial Bank of India (1955)

Soon after Independence, India launched its First Five Year Plan (1951-56). The Plan accorded high priority to the development of rural India, particularly agriculture. The All India Rural Credit Survey Committee recommended the creation of a State-partnered and State-sponsored bank by taking over the Imperial Bank of India and integrating with it the former State-owned or State-associated banks. Accordingly, an Act was passed in the Parliament in May 1955 and the State Bank of India was constituted on July 1, 1955. Later, the State Bank of India (Subsidiary Banks) Act was passed in 1959 enabling the State Bank of India to take over eight former State-associated banks as its subsidiaries.

2.3 Nationalisation of Life Insurance Business (1956)

By the Life Insurance (Emergency Provisions) Ordinance, 1956, promulgated by the President of India on January 19, 1956, the management and control of life insurance business in India, including the foreign business of Indian insurers, and the Indian business of foreign insurers, vested with immediate effect in the Central Government. With this the life insurance business passed from the private sector to the public sector. This was a step never before attempted any where in the world on such a large scale. Though the Ordinance was promulgated in January 1956, the Life Insurance Corporation Act was passed in the next session of parliament. According to this Act the Life Insurance Corporation of India came into existence on September 1, 1956.

2.4 Nationalisation of Commercial Banks (1969 and 1980)

The process of state domination of financial sector was given impetus with the adoption of the policy of social control over banks in 1967, reinforced in 1969 by the nationalisation of 14 major scheduled commercial banks. In April 1980, government nationalised 6 more commercial banks. Driven largely by public sector initiative and policy activism, commercial banks have a dominant share in total financial assets and are the main source of financing for the private corporate sector. They also channel a sizeable share of household savings to the public sector. Besides, in recent years, they have been performing most of the payment system functions. With increased diversification in recent years, banks in both public and private sectors have been providing a wide range of financial services.

2.5 Nationalisation of General Insurance Business (1973)

The general insurance business was nationalized with effect from January 1, 1973, through the General Insurance Business (Nationalization) Act 1972. However, as a prelude to the above Act, the Government took over the management of all the operating companies in 1971 through General Insurance (Emergency Provision) Act, 1971. The emergency Act provided for the appointment of custodians who were empowered to exercise control over these companies subject to the directions of the Central Government. At the time of nationalization of these companies, there were a total of 107 companies underwriting general insurance business in India. All these companies were amalgamated and grouped into four, namely the National Insurance Company Limited, the New India Assurance Company Limited, the Oriental Insurance Company Limited, and the United India Insurance Company Limited with head offices at Kolkata, Mumbai, Delhi and Chennai respectively. The General Insurance Company (GIC) was formed as a holding company in November 1972. The GIC was constituted for the purpose of superintending, controlling and carrying out the business of general insurance. The entire capital of GIC was subscribed by the Government and that of four companies by the GIC on behalf of the Government of India.

Broadly speaking, financial development in India up to the early 1990s was, by and large, a state-induced activity.

2.6 Rethinking on State Domination of Financial Sector

Nationalisation of commercial banks in 1969 and 1980 was a mixed blessing. After nationalisation there was a shift of emphasis from industry to agriculture. The country witnessed rapid expansion in bank branches, even in rural areas. However, bank nationalisation created its own problems like excessive bureaucratisation, red-tapism and disruptive tactics of trade unions of bank employees.

Being a near-monopoly of the Government, the banking sector suffered from lack of competition, low capital base, low productivity and high intermediation cost. The role of technology was minimal and the quality of service was not given adequate importance. Banks also did not follow proper risk management systems and the prudential standards were weak. All these resulted in poor asset quality and low profitability.

Among non-banking financial intermediaries, development finance institutions (DFIs) operated in an over-protected environment with most of the funding coming from assured sources at concessional terms.

The mutual fund industry also suffered from lack of competition and was dominated for long by one institution, viz. the Unit Trust of India (UTI).

Non-banking financial companies (NBFCs) grew rapidly, but there was no regulation regarding their asset side. Financial markets were characterised by control over pricing of financial assets, barriers to entry, high transaction costs and restrictions in movement of funds between the market segments. This, apart from inhibiting the development of the markets, also affected their efficiency.

Similarly, capital market structure in India was subject to several controls and opaque procedures. The trading and settlement system was outdated and not in tune with international practices. Raising of capital from the market was regulated by the Capital Issues (Control) Act, 1947 which was administered by the Controller of Capital Issues (CCIs) in the Ministry of Finance, Government of India. The scheme of controls under the Act required all the companies to obtain prior consent for issues of capital to the public. Pricing as well as the features of the capital structure (such as debt-equity ratios), were controlled by the Government.

The Securities Contracts (Regulation) Act was administered by the Directorate of Stock Exchanges also in the Ministry of Finance. It empowered the Government to recognize and/or derecognise stock exchanges, stipulate rules and bye-laws for their functioning, compel listing of securities by public companies etc. Such a system of regulation and control was fragmented and inadequate in the context of liberalisation wave sweeping across the world. Urgent measures were needed to relax controls and modernise the functioning of capital market.

Furthermore, state monopoly of insurance business resulted in limited availability of insurance products, lack of information technology and poor quality of insurance services. In this connection, the Committee on Reforms in Insurance Sector (Chairman: R.N. Malhotra), which was set up in April 1993 and which submitted its report in January 1994, remarked, "Indian insurance industry lacks depth, diversity and reach, both geographically as well as in terms of insurable population, as there was immensely vast potential yet to be tapped; It provides poor customer service in terms of pricing, adequacy and appropriateness of covers and the much needed and timely claims settlement. It lacks the global dimensions having remained in isolation too long."

In fact, the environment in the financial sector till the initiation of reforms in 1991 was not particularly conducive for the development of deep and wide financial markets. In fact, it had resulted in segmented and underdeveloped markets characterised by paucity of instruments, and limited number of participants. Banks and financial institutions functioned in a highly regulated environment, characterised by an administered interest rate structure, quantitative restrictions on credit flows, fairly high reserve requirements and pre-emption of significant proportion of lendable resources for the priority and Government sectors.

While the quantitative restrictions resulted in credit rationing for the private sector, interest rate controls led to suboptimal use of credit resulting in low levels of investment and growth. These, coupled with other factors such as the absence of proper accounting, transparency and prudential norms, resulted in a large build-up of non-performing assets in the banking system. All this led to erosion of profitability in the banking sector, besides decline in productivity and efficiency. The bank-based and highly controlled regime turned out to be inimical to financial market development.

Thus, until the early 1990s, the role of the financial system in India was primarily restricted to the function of channelling resources from surplus to deficit sectors. Whereas the financial system performed this role reasonably well, its operations came to be marked by some serious deficiencies over the years. The Indian Government determined the quantum, allocation and the price of credit, a situation referred to as *financial repression* by some experts.

It was in this backdrop, that wide-ranging financial sector reforms in India were introduced as an integral part of the economic reforms initiated in the early 1990s.

2.7 Committee on Financial System, 1991

Considering the strategic importance of the financial sector, the Government of India set up a Committee on Financial System in 1991 under the chairmanship of Mr. M. Narasimham. It was asked to examine all aspects relating to the structure, organisation, functions and procedures of the Indian financial system. The Committee submitted its report in November 1991. It was presented to Parliament in December 1991.

Financial sector reforms during the last decade and a half have focused on the following.

- Elimination of segmentation across various markets in order to facilitate transmission of impulses across markets.
- Easing the liquidity management process.
- Making resource allocation more efficient across the economy.

For this purpose, restrictions on pricing of assets have been removed, new instruments have been introduced, and technological infrastructure has been strengthened. In short, liberalisation of the financial sector has included, among others, the following measures.

- Deregulation of interest rates.
- Introduction of new products.
- Relaxation in investment norms for financial intermediaries, especially banks.

- Lowering of restrictions on specialisation/diversification of banks.
- Emergence of new institutions such as primary dealers and mutual funds.
- Withdrawal of reserve requirements on inter-bank borrowings.
- Withdrawal of credit controls and excessively high reserve requirements.
- Deregulation and development of markets.
- Moves toward privatisation of financial services.
- Easing of restrictions in respect of banks' foreign currency investments.
- Easing of restrictions on current and capital account convertibility.
- Lowering of entry barriers/limits on participation of foreign banks.

These reforms have paved the way for integration among various segments of the financial system. It is widely accepted that reduction/removal of financial repression has enhanced the efficiency and potential growth of the Indian economy.

Reforms in the commercial banking sector had two distinct phases. The first phase of reforms introduced subsequent to the release of the Report of the Committee on Financial System (Chairman: M. Narasimham), 1992 focussed mainly on enabling and strengthening measures. The second phase of reforms, introduced subsequent to the recommendations of the Committee on Banking Sector Reforms (Chairman: M. Narasimham), 1998 placed greater emphasis on structural measures and improvement in standards of disclosure and levels of transparency in order to align the Indian standards with international best practices. Reforms have brought about considerable improvements as reflected in various parameters relating to capital adequacy, asset quality, profitability and operational efficiency.

The key objective of reforms in the banking sector in India

has been to enhance the stability and efficiency of banks. To achieve this objective, various reform measures were initiated that could be categorised broadly into three main groups: (a) enabling measures, (b) strengthening measures, and (c) institutional measures.

Enabling measures were designed to create an environment where banks could respond optimally to market signals on the basis of commercial considerations. Salient among these included reduction in statutory pre-emptions so as to release greater funds for commercial lending, interest rate deregulation to enable price discovery, granting of operational autonomy to banks and liberalisation of the entry norms for financial intermediaries.

The strengthening measures aimed at reducing the vulnerability of banks in the face of fluctuations in the economic environment. These included, inter alia, capital adequacy, income recognition, asset classification and provisioning norms, exposure norms, improved levels of transparency, and disclosure standards.

Institutional measures focused on reforms in the legal framework pertaining to banks and creation of new institutions.

2.8 Approach to Financial Sector Reforms

Financial sector reforms in India have formed an important component of the overall economic reforms process initiated in the early 1990s. These reforms have followed a well calibrated approach.

The general approach to financial sector reforms has been a transparent, collaborative and consultative process aimed at resolving many possible dilemmas. The reform process itself was characterised by caution with a tilt towards preserving stability, careful sequencing of measures, mutually reinforcing monetary measures and ensuring consistency and complementarity with other policies.

Further, reforms in the financial markets have been

undertaken within the overall monetary policy framework and in co-ordination with reforms in the money and foreign exchange markets. Many of the major reforms have been implemented in phases, allowing for transition so as not to destabilise market conditions or any group of participants or the financial system in general.

In the context of maximising benefits of financial integration and minimising the risks, the link with the real sector cannot be ignored. In India, reforms in the financial sector started early in the reform cycle which imparted efficiency and stability to the real sector. The financial sector can add competitive strength and growth if reforms in the financial and real sectors keep apace. A major agenda for reform at this juncture for India, given the impressive all-round confidence in the economy, relates to the structure and functioning of institutions and in particular lowering the high transaction costs prevalent in the system. There are several dimensions to the transaction costs—ranging from legal provisions, the judicial system and procedures to attitudes.

The policy of gradualism that has been followed by India focuses on evolution of appropriate institutional framework and the sequencing of reforms based on the experience gained so far. The sequencing and pace of reforms are also vital to safeguard monetary and financial stability and avoid reversals. The issues in this context include: (a) whether bank-based or market-based system of development should be adopted, (b) order of sequencing of reforms of various segments of the financial market to be followed, and (c) whether or not capital account liberalisation should precede domestic financial market reform.

By following a gradualist approach, India has successfully avoided financial disasters as were experienced by some East Asian countries. A number of developing countries especially in Asia that moved early on to the path of economic liberalization had experienced large capital inflows through the 1980s and the first half of the 1990s. Large capital inflows, however, carried the risk of financial sector vulnerability, where the use of such flows is not regulated by application of appropriate mix of macroeconomic and structural policy measures. The recent currency and financial crises in Mexico and Thailand, followed by Korea and Indonesia, provide many insights about the problems that would arise when exchange rates are inflexible, and banking and financial systems are weak.

The experience of the crisis-affected countries highlights the need for setting in place regulatory and supervisory frameworks to ensure the safety and stability of financial systems. Their experience also underscored the premise that financial development is only a necessary condition for sustainable growth, and by no means sufficient. In fact, with the incidence of the costs of financial crises falling on the sovereign governments, financial stability has come to occupy a centre-stage in public policy making along with the requirement of ensuring that the efficiency of the financial sector is high.

Implementation of the reforms process has had several unique features. Financial sector reforms were undertaken early in the reform cycle. Notably, the reforms process was not driven by any banking crisis, nor was it the outcome of any external support package. Besides, the design of the reforms was crafted through domestic expertise, taking on board the international experiences in this respect. The reforms were carefully sequenced with respect to the instruments to be used and the objectives to be achieved.

Thus, prudential norms and supervisory strengthening were introduced early in the reform cycle, followed by interest-rate deregulation and a gradual lowering of statutory pre-emptions. The more complex aspects of legal and accounting measures were ushered in subsequently when the basic tenets of the reforms were already in place.

3

Financial Sector of India: Post-reforms Period

A safe and sound financial sector is a prerequisite for sustained growth of any economy. Globalisation, deregulation and advances in information technology in recent years have brought about significant changes in the operating environment for banks and other financial institutions. These institutions are faced with increased competitive pressures and changing customer demands. These, in turn, have engendered a rapid increase in product innovations and changes in business strategies. While these developments have enabled improvement in the efficiency of financial institutions, they have also posed some serious risks. The regulatory and supervisory policies are, accordingly, being reshaped and reoriented to meet the challenge of containing systemic risks. In this changing milieu, the main challenge for the supervisors has been to maintain the stability of the financial system and, at the same time, provide sufficient flexibility to financial institutions so that they can respond effectively to the growing competition while taking advantage of business opportunities and technological developments.

3.1 Committee on the Financial System, 1991

In the context of the balance of payments crisis of 1991, a comprehensive structural and financial sector reform process was initiated in India as recommended by the Committee on the Financial System (Chairman: M. Narasimham, 1991) which became the starting point for gradual deregulation of the financial sector and development and integration of various segments of the financial market. Measures were initiated to streamline functioning of the financial system to create a sound, competitive and efficient banking system capable of meeting the increasing challenges of liberalisation and globalisation.

With the liberalisation of financial markets, policy authorities in India have also had to contend with episodes of financial volatility as were witnessed in some East Asian countries. Recognising the strong complementarity between financial stability and macroeconomic stability, the operational settings for policies are being geared to dampen excessive volatility and the possible impairment of the ability of financial institutions to handle fluctuations in financial asset prices. Current macroeconomic and financial developments in the Indian economy highlight the evolving role of the financial sector in the functioning of the economy and the growing integration across financial markets.

The financial sector in the Indian economy is undergoing a transformation towards a vibrant, competitive and diversified system, with a multiplicity of financial institutions having different risk profiles intermediating in various segments of the market spectrum. The development of banking is a critical element in the agenda of financial sector reforms in India.

Financial sector reforms in India are by no means complete. Plans are afoot to modernise the financial system to make it compatible with best international practices. Reforms in the financial sector are wide-ranging, encompassing institutional, legal and technological aspects of the functioning of financial intermediaries and financial markets.

3.2 Developing and Strengthening Financial Infrastructure

Measures to improve market infrastructure must be implemented at an early stage of reform alongside appropriate legal framework. These conditions facilitate growth of financial transactions including inter-bank transactions and active liquidity management.

Presence of well-established institutions, soundness of bank balance sheets, existence of adequate safety nets and vigilant supervision are the pre-requisites for successful financial liberalisation. The reform process in India within the banking system has sought to strengthen the balance sheets of individual banks, empower banks to respond in the most optimal manner to market stimuli and to establish institutions to ensure a level playing field for all market participants and provide a back-up system for contingencies.

Competition has been infused into the financial system by licensing new private banks since 1993. Foreign banks have also been given more liberal entry.

Progress has also been generated through demonstration and spread effects of advanced technology and risk management practices accompanying new private banks and foreign banks. Given the fiscal constraint being faced by the Government and in keeping with the evolving principles of corporate governance, the Government permitted public sector banks to raise fresh equity from markets to meet their capital shortfalls or to expand their lending. Several public and private sector banks have accessed the domestic equity market. Public sector banks have also raised capital through GDR/ADRs while many banks have raised subordinated debt through the private placement route.

3.3 Financial Regulation and Supervision

The quality of financial regulation and supervision as well as of information and the legal system are important for reaping the benefits of globalisation. Hence, enactment of enabling legislation has been a priority area of the reforms. The Board for Financial Supervision (BFS) was constituted in 1994, with the mandate to exercise the powers of supervision and inspection in relation to the banking companies, financial institutions and non-banking financial companies.

With the switchover to international best practices on income recognition, asset classification and provisioning, the problem of non-performing assets (NPAs) assumed critical importance. It was widely perceived that the level of NPAs in

India was high by international standards. The problem needed to be tackled urgently and from different fronts. A menu approach has been adopted to tackle this major constraint confronting the banking sector. These policy measures have resulted in reduction in gross NPAs in the banking system.

The need for monitoring and supervising becomes even more important systemically with the opening up of the economy. Thus, the prudential regulations were fortified by reorientation of *on-site inspections* and introduction of *off-site surveillance*. The focus of inspection has shifted from ensuring appropriate credit planning and credit allocation under a closed economy framework to assessment of the bank's safety and soundness and to identify areas where corrective action is needed to strengthen the institution and improve its performance.

In view of the growing liberalisation of the external sector and international banking by banks in India, monitoring of the cross-border flow of funds has assumed importance. RBI now compiles and disseminates international banking statistics (IBS) on the lines of the reporting system devised by the Bank for International Settlements (BIS). The locational banking statistics (LBS) provide the gross position of international assets and international liabilities of all banking offices located in India. They report exclusively banks' international transactions including the transactions with any of their own branches/subsidiaries/joint ventures located outside India.

3.4 Financial Openness

In India, opening up of the financial sector in terms of entry of foreign entities and easing of restrictions on international transactions took place within the broader process of reforms. The constant policy concern in this respect has been that of preparing the financial sector for global competition and taking preventive measures for the potential vulnerabilities that it might engender.

Despite their extensive branch network, the biggest banks

in India are miniscule compared to most multinational banks, in terms of standard parameters like assets or deposits. Hence, the initial focus of reforms in the financial sector was to strengthen the domestic financial infrastructure, make it more competitive and to provide banks greater freedom in their foreign operations.

Since 1991, the presence of foreign entities within the Indian banking sector has increased and so also the international transactions of Indian banks.

International experience has shown that the cost of financial intermediation declines and quality of financial services improves with opening of the economy. However, openness should be preceded by deregulation and strengthening of institutional framework in order to limit contagious influences. The strategy adopted in India has been to maximise the beneficial effects of openness while minimising the adverse consequences. Financial crises due to internal/external factors have been averted, while the financial system has been progressively deregulated and strengthened.

3.5 International Security Standards

There are at present a number of security standards available for different financial applications. Most of them are internationally accepted and part of the ISO standards. These international standards such as the BS7799 [1] have been accepted by the RBI. Banks, however, could also put in place measures which conform to their own policies and ensure regular and periodical audit.

The objectives of these standards are as listed below.

- To provide management direction and support for information security, which is a basic pre-requisite for BS7799.
- To manage information security within the organisation, maintain the security of organisational information processing facilities and information assets accessed by third parties, and to maintain the security of information

when the responsibility for information processing has been outsourced to another organisation.

- To maintain appropriate protection of corporate assets and ensure that information assets receive an appropriate level of protection.
- To reduce risks of human error, theft, fraud or misuse of facilities and minimise the damage from security incidents and malfunctions and learn from such incidents.
- To ensure the correct and secure operation of information processing facilities, minimise the risk of systems failures, to protect the integrity of software and information and maintain the integrity and availability of information processing and communication.
- To control access to information, prevent unauthorised access, detect unauthorised activities and ensure information security when using mobile computing and tele-networking facilities.
- To ensure security is built into operational systems, to prevent loss, modification or misuse of user data in application systems.
- To counteract interruptions to business activities and critical business processes from the effects of major failures or disasters.
- To prevent breaches of any criminal or civil law, statutory, regulatory or contractual obligations and of any security requirements, ensure compliance of systems with organisational security policies and standards and minimise interference to/from the system audit process.

3.6 Migration to Basel III Norms

The banking systems worldwide are migrating to the Basel III regime. Basel III is a comprehensive set of reform measures, developed by the Basel Committee on Banking Supervision, to strengthen the regulation, supervision and risk management of the banking sector.

These measures aim to:

(a) improve the banking sector's ability to absorb shocks arising from financial and economic stress, whatever the source may be;

(b) improve risk management and governance; and

(c) strengthen banks' transparency and disclosures.

The Reserve Bank of India had issued guidelines on implementation of Basel III capital regulation in India on May 2, 2012. These guidelines were to be implemented as on January 1, 2013 in a phased manner and were to be fully implemented as on March 31, 2018. However, the Reserve Bank of India has rescheduled the start date for implementation of Basel III to April 1, 2013.

To quote RBI governor Duvvuri Subbarao, "Basel III represents an effort to fix the gaps and lacunae in Basel II that came to light during the crisis as also to reflect other lessons of the crisis. What is important though is that Basel III does not jettison Basel II; on the contrary, it builds on the essence of Basel II—the link between the risk profiles and capital requirements of individual banks. In that sense, Basel III is not a negation, but an enhancement of Basel II.

The enhancements of Basel III over Basel II come primarily in four areas: (i) augmentation in the level and quality of capital; (ii) introduction of liquidity standards; (iii) modifications in provisioning norms; and (iv) better and more comprehensive disclosures".

3.7 Accounting and Auditing Standards

Indian accounting standards are generally in alignment with international accounting standards, except for some modifications to suit local customs, usages and level of development in the country. There has been significant progress in accounting standards though some issues remain to be addressed. There are suggestions that Institute of Chartered Accountants of India (ICAI) needs to be made an autonomous body with its own staff and independent funding. Need has also been felt to develop country-specific/sector-specific standards where similar standards are not developed by International Accounting Standards Board (IASB). Similarly, ICAI should make attempts to attain convergence with International Financial Reporting Standards (IFRS).

India is one of the earliest countries to have adopted International Standards on Auditing by amending them to suit Indian requirements. There has been significant progress since ROSC-2004. However, there are some areas which need attention. Auditing and Assurance Standards Board (AASB) needs to take steps to attain convergence with International Standards on Auditing. It needs to take proactive steps by bringing out more technical guidance and other literature to help small and medium practitioners to understand standards. There is a need to give functional independence to AASB.

3.7.1 Marking-to-market: The Indian accounting standards are generally aligned to the International Financial Reporting Standards, though there are some differences. India is yet to fully adopt the marking-to-market requirements as available in the international standards. The Indian standards are relatively conservative and do not permit recognition of unrealised gains in the profit and loss account or equity, though unrealised losses are required to be accounted. Banks are required to mark-to-market the investments in the Held for Trading (HFT) and Available for Sale (AFS) categories at periodical intervals, on a portfolio basis, and provide for the net losses and ignore the net gains. This has proved to be a stabilising factor, inasmuch as it has not induced an imbalance in the incentive structures and has also proved to be less pro-cyclical.

3.8 Technological Solutions for Financial Services

Most of the initiatives regarding technology are aimed at providing better and more efficient customer service by offering multiple options to the customer. The death of distance, which is a by-product of technology, has become a reality in the banking sector. Technology is also playing a key role in banks' strategy for gaining a competitive edge.

Many banks have commenced the process of setting up core banking solutions, which are at various stages of implementation. While such systems are already in place in respect of new private sector banks, a few old private sector banks and public sector banks are also quickly moving to set up such processes. This would benefit the customer in the banking sector. Computerisation of the business of banks has been receiving high importance. The public sector banks have already crossed the 70 percent level of computerisation of their business. The directive from the Central Vigilance Commission (CVC) to achieve 100 percent computerisation has resulted in renewed vigour towards computerisation of branches.

Networking has been receiving focused attention by banks. This activity is also being monitored by the RBI. Most banks have their own corporate networks to facilitate inter-branch and branch-controlling office communication in an electronic mode. Inter-bank and inter-city communication takes place through the Indian Financial Network (INFINET). As part of the INFINET, the terrestrial lines have been augmented to provide for increased data transfer capabilities. All these have resulted in the dependence of banks on network-based computing which has benefited the customer.

INFINET also provides for safe and secure transmission of electronic messages with the use of public key infrastructure (PKI) which has the legal backing of Information Technology Act, 2000. It also provides for messages to flow in a structured environment, using the structured financial messaging solutions (SFMS), which provides for inter-operability of messages so that straight through processing (STP) is achieved.

Another major development witnessed in recent years is the growth in multiple delivery channels to customers such as internet-based banking, mobile banking and anywhere banking. This has benefited the customers and the banks alike.

While customers have now a wide variety of options to choose from, banks have been able to reduce costs which have had a positive impact on their profitability.

These developments have, however, also posed certain challenges. In a world where geographical barriers are losing significance, it is essential that security is given prime importance in a trans-national scenario where large sums of money are at stake. While the challenges relating to physical security could be confronted with relative ease, the position is much more complicated in respect of IT security. The RBI has, therefore, provided guidelines on information system (IS) security as also IS audit which banks can use for their benefit. These are generic in nature and do not have any prescriptive tones.

3.9 Legal Reforms for Strengthening Financial Sector

An efficient financial system requires a regulatory framework with well-defined objectives, adequate and clear legal framework and transparent supervisory procedure. This, in turn, requires comprehensive legislations to enable the regulatory authorities to discharge their responsibilities effectively. The RBI has, therefore, been making constant efforts to upgrade and strengthen the legal framework in tune with the changing environment.

3.9.1 Recent Acts Enacted by the Parliament: The Enforcement of Security Interest and Recovery Debts Laws (Amendment) Act, 2004 (Act No. 30 of 2004) was amended the Securitisation and Reconstruction of Financial Assets and Enforcement of Security Interest Act, 2002 (SARFAESI), the Recovery of Debts Due to Banks and Financial Institutions Act, 1993 and the Companies Act, 1956. By this amendment Act, the SARFAESI Act was amended to provide, *inter alia,* for the following.

- Enable the borrower to make an application before the Debt Recovery Tribunal against the measures taken by the secured creditor without depositing any portion of the money due.

- Provide that the Debt Recovery Tribunal shall dispose of the application as expeditiously as possible within a period of 60 days from the date of application.
- Enable any person aggrieved by any order made by the Debt Recovery Tribunal to file an appeal before the Debt Recovery Appellate Tribunal after depositing with the Appellate Tribunal 50 percent of the amount of debt due from him as claimed by the secured creditor or as determined by the Debt Recovery Tribunal, whichever is less.

3.9.2 Credit Information Companies (Regulation) Act, 2005: It is aimed at providing for regulation of credit information companies and to facilitate efficient distribution of credit. No company can commence or carry on the business of credit information without obtaining a certificate of registration from the RBI. The Act sets out procedures for obtaining certificate of registration, the requirements of minimum capital and management of credit information companies. The Act also empowers the RBI to determine policy in relation to functioning of credit information companies and to give directions to such companies, credit institutions and specified users.

The Act also lays down the functions of credit information companies, powers and duties of auditors, obtaining of membership by credit institutions in credit information companies, information privacy principles, alterations of credit information files and credit reports, regulation of unauthorised access to credit information, offences and penalties, obligations as to fidelity and secrecy.

Other salient features of the Act include settlement of disputes between credit institutions and credit information companies or between credit institutions and their borrowers. The Act also provides for amendment of certain enactments so as to permit disclosure of credit information.

3.9.3 Government Securities Act, 2006: This Act was enacted by the Parliament with a view to consolidating and amending the law relating to Government securities and its management by the Reserve Bank of India. The Act applies to Government securities created and issued, whether before or after the commencement of the Act, by the Central or a State Government. Accordingly, the Public Debt Act, 1944 ceased to apply to the Government securities. The Indian Securities Act, 1920 was repealed.

The new Act would facilitate widening and deepening of the Government securities market and its more effective regulation by the Reserve Bank in various ways, such as:

- Stripping or reconstitution of Government securities.
- Legal recognition of beneficial ownership of the investors in Government securities through the Constituents' Subsidiary General Ledger (CSGL).
- Statutory backing for the Reserve Bank's power to debar Subsidiary General Ledger (SGL) account holders from trading, either temporarily or permanently, for misuse of SGL account facility.
- Facility of pledge or hypothecation or lien of Government securities for availing of loan.
- Extension of nomination facility to hold the securities or receive the amount thereof in the event of death of the holder.
- Recognition of title to Government security of the deceased holder on the basis of documents other than succession certificate such as will executed by the deceased holder, registered deed of family settlement, gift deed, deed of partition, etc., as prescribed by the Reserve Bank of India.
- Recognition of mother as the guardian of the minor for the purpose of holding Government Securities.
- Statutory powers to the Reserve Bank to call for information, cause inspection and issue directions in relation to Government securities.

3.9.4 Payment and Settlement Systems Act, 2007: This Act, along with Payment and Settlement Systems Regulations, 2008, stipulates that no person other than the Reserve Bank of

India (RBI), shall commence or operate a payment system except under and in accordance with an authorisation issued by the RBI under the provisions of the Act.

All persons currently operating a payment system or desirous of setting up a payment system, as defined in Section 2(1)(i) of the Act should apply for authorisation to the Reserve Bank, unless specifically exempted in terms of the Act. Existing payment systems will cease to have the right to carry on their operations, unless they obtain an authorisation within six months from the commencement of the Act (i.e. August 12, 2008).

The Payment and Settlement Systems Regulations, 2008 detail the form and manner in which the application is to be made to the Reserve Bank for grant of authorisation.

3.10 Committee on Financial Sector Reforms, 2008

It made the following recommendations:

- Allow more entry to private well-governed, deposit-taking small finance banks.
- Liberalise the banking correspondent regulation so that a wide range of local agents can serve to extend financial services. Use technology both to reduce costs and to limit fraud and misrepresentation.
- Offer priority sector loan certificates (PSLC) to all entities that lend to eligible categories in the priority sector. Allow banks that undershoot their priority sector obligations to buy the PSLC and submit it towards fulfilment of their target.
- Sell small under-performing public sector banks, possibly to another bank or to a strategic investor, to gain experience with the process and gauge outcomes.
- Create stronger boards for large public sector banks, with more power to outside shareholders (including possibly a private sector strategic investor), devolving the power to appoint and compensate top executives to the board.
- After starting the process of strengthening boards, delink

the banks from additional government oversight, including by the Central Vigilance Commission and Parliament, with the justification that with government-controlled boards governing the banks, a second layer of oversight is not needed.
- Be more liberal in allowing takeovers and mergers, including by domestically incorporated subsidiaries of foreign banks.
- Free banks to set up branches and ATMs anywhere.

3.11 Committee on Financial Sector Assessment (CFSA), 2009

In March 2009, the Government and RBI jointly released the report of the Committee on Financial Sector Assessment (CFSA) that was co-chaired by Deputy Governor Rakesh Mohan and Finance Secretary Ashok Chawla. The report is the culmination of work started in September 2006 to undertake a comprehensive self-assessment of India's financial sector, particularly focusing on stability assessment and stress testing and compliance with all financial standards and codes.

CFSA owed its origins to the Financial Sector Assessment Programme (FSAP) that was initiated in 1999 and carried out jointly by the IMF and the World Bank after the Asian crisis. Several countries, including India, participated in this long-drawn and resource-intensive exercise. This programme so far has been conducted by the IMF and the World Bank using experts from around the world to carry out the assessment with participation from the host country.

The CFSA followed a forward-looking and holistic approach to self-assessment, based on three mutually reinforcing pillars:

- Financial stability assessment and stress testing.
- Legal, infrastructural and market development issues.
- Assessment of the status of implementation of international financial standards and codes.

The first pillar is essentially concerned with stability assessment. Taking into account the legal, regulatory and supervisory architecture in India, the CFSA felt the need for involving, and associating closely, all the major regulatory institutions in the financial sector—RBI, SEBI and IRDA, besides the relevant government departments. Direct official involvement at different levels brought about enormous responsibility, ownership, and commitment to the process, ensuring constructive pragmatism when faced with contentious issues.

Since the assessment required comprehensive domain knowledge in the various technical areas examined, the CFSA initially constituted Technical Groups comprising officials with first-hand experience in handling the respective areas from the regulatory agencies concerned as well as the government to undertake the preliminary assessment and to prepare technical notes and background material in the concerned areas. This ensured that officials who are well-conversant with their own systems and are aware of the existing strengths and weaknesses could identify the best alternative solutions.

To ensure an impartial assessment, the CFSA constituted four external independent Advisory Panels, comprising non-official experts drawn from within the country. These Panels made their assessments after thorough debate and rigorous scrutiny of inputs provided by the Technical Groups. To further strengthen the credibility of this assessment, the Advisory Panels' assessments were reviewed by eminent international experts.

The CFSA then drew up its own overview report at the final stage, drawing upon the assessments, findings and recommendations of the Advisory Panels and the comments of the peer reviewers. The assessments and recommendations comprise six volumes.

Overall, the CFSA found that India's financial system is essentially sound and resilient, and that systemic stability is by and large robust. India is broadly compliant with most of the standards and codes though gaps were noted in the timely implementation of bankruptcy proceedings.

Of immediate interest, and related closely to the current macroeconomic conditions, the CFSA also carried out single-factor stress-tests for credit and market risks and liquidity ratio and scenario analyses. These tests show that there are no significant vulnerabilities in the banking system. This does not mean that NPAs will not rise in this economic slowdown. NPAs may indeed rise. However, given the strength of the banks' balance sheets, that rise is not likely to pose any systemic risks, as it might in many advanced countries.

Risk assessment, however, is a continuous process and the stress tests need to be conducted taking into account the macroeconomic linkages as also the second round and contagion risks.

3.12 Achievements of Financial Sector Reforms

Financial sector in the Indian economy since the early 1990s has undergone a transformation towards a vibrant, competitive and diversified system, with a multiplicity of financial institutions having different risk profiles intermediating in various segments of the market spectrum. The evolution of the Indian financial system from somewhat of a constricted and an undersized one to a more open, deregulated and market oriented one and its interface with the growth process are the major areas of reforms still underway.

The financial system has exhibited considerable dynamism in recent years. The system today is varied, with a well-diversified structure of financial institutions, financial companies and mutual funds. The setting up of some specialised financial institutions and refinance institutions has provided depth to financial intermediation outside the banking sector. These developments, coupled with increased financial market liberalization, have enhanced competition. A number of existing financial institutions have diversified into several new activities, such as, investment banking and infrastructure financing, providing guarantees for domestic and offshore lending for infrastructure projects.

Rapid expansion of non-banking financial companies (NBFCs) has taken place, providing avenues for depositors to hold assets and for borrowers to enhance the scale of funding of their activities. Various types of NBFCs have provided varied services that include equipment leasing, hire purchase, loans, investments, mutual benefit and chit fund activities. More recently, NBFCs activity has picked up in the area of housing finance.

Financial development is also reflected in the growing importance of mutual funds. In the 1990s, they enabled sizable mobilisation of financial surpluses of the households for investment in capital markets. Capital markets themselves have become an important source of financing corporate investments, especially after firms were permitted to charge share premium in a flexible manner.

An understanding of the organisational structure of markets for financial assets is vital for knowing the limitations and prospects with regards to efficiency, integration and stability. Financial markets in India comprise, in the main: the credit market, the money market, the foreign exchange market, the debt market and the capital market. Recently, the derivatives market has also emerged. With banks having already been allowed to undertake insurance business, bancassurance market is also likely to emerge in a big way.

Most of the financial markets were characterised, till the early 1990s, by controls over the pricing of financial assets, restrictions on flows or transactions, barriers to entry, low liquidity and high transaction costs. These characteristics came in the way of development of the markets and allocative efficiency of resources channelled through them.

The initiation of financial sector reforms in the early 1990s was essentially to bring about a transformation in the structure, efficiency and stability of financial markets, as also an integration of the markets.

3.13 Areas of Concern

In spite of the significant improvements in the banking industry as a result of reforms, several challenges lie ahead, the most important being the need to bring down the NPAs. Commercial banks continue to face the problem of non-performing assets (NPAs), attributable, inter alia, to factors such as weak debt recovery mechanism, non-realisation of collateral and poor credit appraisal techniques. Policy measures have not yielded the desired results. The recent enactment of the Securitisation and Reconstruction of Financial Assets and Enforcement of Security Interest Act, 2002 has increased the momentum for the recovery of NPAs. However, banks need to intensify their efforts to recover their overdues and prevent generation of fresh NPAs.

Co-operative banks constitute an important segment of the Indian banking system. They have an extensive branch network and reach out to people in remote areas. They have traditionally played an important role in creating banking habits among the lower and middle-income groups and in strengthening the rural credit delivery system. Unfortunately, financial reforms have not impacted the functioning of co-operative banks. Since the introduction of reforms, there has been very little perceptible improvement in either stability or efficiency of co-operative banks. In particular, the asset quality and profitability of co-operative banks has shown some deterioration in the reform period. Positive impact of reforms, as has been witnessed in the case of commercial banking sector, may take longer to get manifested for co-operative banks given the late start of the reform process in this sector.

Financial institutions, which constitute an important source of funds for the commercial sector, have been losing ground fast. The situation has come about as a result of the distinction between development and commercial banking getting blurred, high cost of funds and asset-liability mismatches. With reforms in the financial sector, the facility of low cost funds under long-term operations funds, funds from bilateral and multilateral agencies and bond issues under statutory liquidity ratio is no more available. Now the financial institutions are raising funds at market-related rates of interest. The Reserve Bank of India (RBI) has been advising financial institutions to chart a path for their evolution into universal banks. The merger of ICICI with the ICICI Bank was approved by the RBI in April 2002.

Competitive pressures as well as prudential regulatory requirements have made banks risk-averse, preferring their investment in relatively risk-free gilt instruments. The behaviour and strategies of bank business would need to change from the present so that they can factor in their own risk assessment even while performing their core activities. There is a need to ensure long term finance to support development and growth in the economy, even as restructuring takes place through mergers and universal banking.

True, there has been a significant progress towards globalisation in the recent past in India, the extent to which the country is globalised is considerably low as compared with other emerging economies. This indicates not only the existence of enormous opportunities but also challenges in terms of transition from a non-entity to a major player in the global financial system.

To conclude, India's financial sector has made rapid strides in reforming itself and aligning itself to the new competitive business environment. While the operational and supervisory practices in the sector have progressively approximated international best practices, the process of convergence is not yet complete. Greater conformity to prudential norms of international standards as also adoption of better systems of risk management will enhance the stability of the financial system even as banks expand the range and volume of their operations.

End Note

1. BS7799 is comprehensive in its coverage of security issues, containing a significant number of control requirements. Hence,

compliance with it is a major task for most organisations. By following this standard, financial institutions including banks can ensure compliance to most of the information security requirements.

4

Capital Market: Evolution and Present Structure

Capital market plays a very important role in the development of financial system of any economy. It is a market where financial assets such as equities or debt are traded over a long period of time. It is an important source of raising long-term funds both by government as well as by corporates. Capital market comprises of primary market and secondary market. Primary market is a market wherein companies raise new funds in the form of debt or equity and financial institutions invest in these securities.

On the other hand, in secondary markets, securities once issued in primary market are traded among investors or traders on the recognized stock exchanges. Every country has a regulator of capital market which regulates the activities in such markets and also safeguards investors' interest. Securities and Exchange Board of India (SEBI), set up in 1992, is the regulator for Indian capital market.

4.1 Capital Market: Meaning and Significance

Capital market is a market for long-term funds. The distinction between capital market and money market is not watertight. Broadly speaking, capital market focuses on financing of fixed investment (machinery and equipment) while money market provides working capital finance (raw material etc.)

Capital market channelises household savings to the corporate sector and allocates funds to firms. In this process, it allows both firms and households to share risks associated with business. Moreover, capital market enables the valuation of firms on an almost continuous basis and plays an important role in the governance of the corporate sector.

An efficient capital market is an important constituent of a sound financial system. In India, efforts have been made in recent years to set up an effective regulatory framework covering major participants in the capital market. Similarly, the technology of trading and settlements in the stock exchanges has been upgraded. Internet-based trading in securities has been permitted. Foreign institutional investors (FIIs) and pension funds were allowed to enter the Indian stock market from 1993 onwards. The market has undergone a major transformation in terms of its structure, products, practices, spread, institutional framework and other important aspects like transparency, integrity and efficiency since then. The size of the market has also grown manifold.

The capital market fosters economic growth in the following ways:

- It augments the quantum of savings and capital formation in the economy.
- It allocates capital efficiently thereby raising the productivity of investment.
- It enhances the efficiency of a financial system as diverse competitors vie with each other for financial resources.
- It adds to the financial deepening of the economy by enlarging the financial sector and promoting the use of innovative, sophisticated and cost-effective financial instruments, which ultimately reduce the cost of capital.
- Well-functioning capital markets also impose discipline on firms to perform.
- Equity and debt markets stress on the banking sector by diversifying credit risk across the economy.

4.2 Capital Market in the Pre-1991 Period

Historically, different kinds of financial intermediaries have existed in the Indian financial system. At the time of Independence in 1947, working capital requirements of corporates were financed mainly by commercial banks. As the capital market was underdeveloped, a number of development finance institutions (DFIs) were set up at the all-India and the State levels to meet the long-term fund requirements of companies.

Prior to the onset of financial sector reforms in 1991, the capital market structure in India was subject to several controls and opaque procedures. The objective of control over capital issues was to channel the limited capital resources available for investment in the country into desired areas. Apart from this main objective, capital issues control was put to several other uses, these being the following:

- Regulation of bonus issues.
- Regulation of terms and conditions of foreign capital participation in Indian companies and the regulation of the terms and conditions of dilution or repatriation of foreign equity.
- Regulation of capital re-organisation plans of companies, including mergers and amalgamations.
- Regulation of the capital structure of companies, as well as the terms and conditions of additional issues.
- Regulation of the volume and timing of the private issue of capital.

Moreover, the trading and settlement system was outdated and not in tune with international practices. Raising of capital from the market was regulated by the Capital Issues (Control) Act, 1947 which was administered by the Controller of Capital Issues (CCIs) in the Ministry of Finance, Government of India. The scheme of controls under the Act required all the companies to obtain prior consent for issues of capital to the public. Pricing as well as the features of the capital structure (such as debt-equity ratios), were controlled by the Government. Similarly, the Securities Contracts (Regulation) Act, 1956 was administered by the Directorate of Stock Exchanges also in the Ministry of Finance. It empowered the Government to recognise/derecognise stock exchanges, stipulate rules and by-laws for their functioning, compel listing of securities by public companies etc. Such a system of regulation and control was fragmented and inadequate in the context of liberalisation wave sweeping across the world. Urgent measures were needed to relax controls and modernise the functioning of capital market.

Capital market structure has evolved over time with the market practices and conditions generally reflecting the policies put in place. Till the onset of reforms in the early 1990s, raising of resources in the primary segment of the market was subject to several controls, disallowing pricing to be determined by market conditions. Trading in the secondary market was subject to opaque practices. The trading and settlement system was outdated and out of tune with internationally followed practices. The volumes, however, increased and securities continued to exist in physical form. Physical securities also created uncertainties for investors and increased the transaction costs. Besides, long and uncertain settlement cycles created serious problems for clearing houses. Informational flows to the market participants were also deficient. It was considered necessary to orient the SEBI to undertake the tasks of regulation and supervision. The SEBI was, for this purpose, given statutory powers through a separate legislation in 1992.

4.3 Securities and Exchange Board of India (SEBI)

In 1992, the Capital Issues (Control) Act, 1947 was repealed and the office of the Controller of Capital Issues (CCIs) was abolished.

The Securities and Exchange Board of India (SEBI) was constituted on April 12, 1988 as a non-statutory body through an Administrative Resolution of the Government for dealing with all matters relating to development and regulation of the securities market and investor protection and to advise the government on all these matters. SEBI was given statutory status and powers through an Ordinance promulgated on January 30, 1992. SEBI was established as a statutory body on

February 21, 1992. The Ordinance was replaced by Securities and Exchange Board of India Act, 1992 on April 4, 1992.

With this ended all controls related to raising of funds from the market. The move was aimed at enhancing the efficiency, safety, integrity and transparency of the market. Presently, Issuers of capital are required to meet the guidelines of SEBI on disclosures and protection of investors.

4.3.1 Objectives: SEBI has emerged as an autonomous and independent statutory body. Its legally mandated objectives are the following:

- Protection of the interests of investors in securities.
- Development of the securities market.
- Regulation of the securities market.
- Matters connected therewith and incidental thereto.

The SEBI prohibits fraudulent and unfair trade practices, including insider trading. It also regulates substantial acquisition of shares and takeovers. In order to ensure protection of investors and to safeguard the integrity of the markets, there is a comprehensive surveillance system. Stock exchanges are the primary targets for detection of market manipulation, price rigging and other regulatory breaches regarding capital market functioning.

The SEBI regulates and supervises the securities market through its various regulations, guidelines and schemes issued from time to time.

4.3.2 Powers and Functions: The powers and functions of SEBI—as the securities market regulator—have been laid down in the SEBI Act, 1992. SEBI also exercises powers under the Securities Contracts (Regulation) Act, 1956, the Depositories Act, 1996 and certain provisions of the Companies Act, 1956. It regulates the securities markets, securities market institutions and market intermediaries, such as the stock exchanges, depositories, mutual funds and other asset management companies, securities dealers and brokers, merchant bankers, credit rating agencies and venture capital funds.

The statutory powers and functions of SEBI were strengthened through the promulgation of the Securities Laws (Amendment) Ordinance on January 25, 1995, which was subsequently replaced by an Act of Parliament.

The SEBI is equipped with the following powers:

- Powers to register and regulate, inspect, enquire and investigate and undertake audits, and to cancel registration (though in this last case this applies to the mutual fund rather than the AMC); also to prohibit issue of an offer document including prospectus or advertisement.
- Powers to summon and enforce attendance and examine on oath, inspect registers and documents, discover and enforce disclosure of books of account and other documents.
- Powers to restrain from business, suspend, search, impound and retain proceeds, access bank data and attach bank accounts, prevent alienation of assets and issue cease and desist orders.
- Powers to require compensation to be paid to investors.

Those who appeal against SEBI judgements are heard by the Securities Appellate Tribunal (SAT) and can also go to the Supreme Court if they do not accept the Tribunal's judgement. The SAT has three members, one of whom is required to be the presiding officer who is a sitting or retired judge of the Supreme Court or High Court. The two other members must be of ability, integrity and standing with experience of corporate law, securities law, finance, economics or accountancy.

SEBI has around 650+ staff and regional offices in five cities—Mumbai, New Delhi, Chennai, Kolkata and Ahmedabad.

4.3.3 Organisational Strengthening of SEBI: The experience of SEBI during episodes of market misconduct revealed many limitations in the legal provisions of the SEBI Act. In addition, the growing importance of the securities markets in the economy has placed new demands upon SEBI.

On October 28, 2002, an ordinance was promulgated which sought to strengthen SEBI. This ordinance involved organisational strengthening of SEBI, giving SEBI more powers for investigations and penalties, and making clearer concepts like insider trading and market manipulations.

The regulatory ambit has been widened in tune with the emerging needs and developments in the equity markets. Apart from stock exchanges, various intermediaries such as mutual funds, stock brokers and sub-brokers, merchant bankers, portfolio managers, registrars to an issue, share transfer agents, underwriters, debentures trustees, bankers to an issue, custodian of securities, venture capital funds and issuers have been brought under the SEBI's regulatory purview.

Since 1992, foreign institutional investors (FIIs) are permitted to invest in all types of securities, including corporate debt and government securities in stages and subject to limits. Further, the Indian corporate sector was allowed to access international capital markets through American Depository Receipts (ADRs), Global Depository Receipts (GDRs), Foreign Currency Convertible Bonds (FCCBs) and External Commercial Borrowings (ECBs). Eligible foreign companies have been permitted to raise money from domestic capital markets through issue of Indian Depository Receipts (IDRs).

Regulations governing substantial acquisition of shares and takeovers of companies have also been put in place. These are aimed at making the takeover process more transparent and to protect the interests of minority shareholders.

To sustain confidence in clearing and settlement of securities, NSE set up the National Securities Clearing Corporation Ltd. (NSCCL) in August, 1995 which carries out the clearing and settlement of the trades executed in the equities and derivatives segments and operates the Subsidiary General Ledger (SGL) for settlement of trades in government securities. Similarly, the BSE has its own clearing house.

The equity market has witnessed wide-spread development

in infrastructure and its functioning is comparable to international standards. It has seen significant increase in growth and diversity in composition since early 1990s.

Trading infrastructure in the stock exchanges has been modernised by replacing the open outcry system with on-line screen-based electronic trading. This has improved the liquidity in the Indian capital market and led to better price discovery. The trading and settlement cycles were initially shortened from 14 days to 7 days. Subsequently, to enhance the efficiency of the secondary market, rolling settlement was introduced on a T+5 basis. With effect from April 1, 2002, the settlement cycle for all listed securities was shortened to T+3 and further to T+2 from April 1, 2003. Shortening of settlement cycles helped in reducing risks associated with unsettled trades due to market fluctuations.

As a result of these initiatives, there has been a significant rise in the volume of transactions and the emergence of new and innovative instruments. In addition to the two national stock exchanges, viz., the NSE and BSE, there are 17 regional stock exchanges. The importance of regional stock exchanges, however, has been on the decline in recent times.

However, the role of equity market in capital formation continues to be limited. The private corporate debt market is active mainly in the form of private placements, while the public issue market for corporate debt is yet to pick up. It is the primary equity and debt markets that link the issuers of securities and investors and provide resources for capital formation. A growing economy requires risk capital and long-term resources in the form of debt for enabling the corporates to choose an appropriate mix of debt and equity. Long-term resources are also important for financing infrastructure projects. Therefore, in order to sustain India's high growth path, the capital market needs to play a major role. The significance of a well-functioning domestic capital market has also increased as banks need to raise necessary capital from the market to sustain their growing operations.

4.4 Summing Up

To sum up, the Indian capital market has become modern in terms of market infrastructure and trading and settlement practices. The capital market has also become a much safer place than it was before the reform process began. The secondary capital market in India has also become deep and liquid. There has also been a reduction in transaction costs and significant improvement in efficiency and transparency. However, the role of the domestic capital market in capital formation in the country, both directly and indirectly through mutual funds, continues to be less significant.

Although the capital market in India has a long history, during the most part, it remained on the periphery of the financial system. Various reforms undertaken since the early 1990s by the Securities and Exchange Board of India (SEBI) and the Government have brought about a significant structural transformation in the Indian capital market. As a result, the Indian equity market has become modern and transparent.

The improvement in clearing and settlement system has brought a substantial reduction in transaction costs. Several measures were also undertaken to enhance the safety and integrity of the market. These include capital requirements, trading and exposure limits, daily margins comprising mark-to-market margins and VaR based margins. Trade/settlement guarantee fund has also been set up to ensure smooth settlement of transactions in case of default by any member. Another important development of the reform process was the opening up of mutual funds industry to the private sector in 1992, which earlier was the monopoly of the Unit Trust of India (UTI) and mutual funds set up by public sector financial institutions.

5

Capital Market Reforms

The Indian equity market has witnessed a series of reforms since the early 1990s. The reforms have been implemented in a gradual and sequential manner, based on international best practices and modified to suit the needs of the country. The reform measures were aimed at the following:

- Creating growth-enabling institutions.
- Boosting competitive conditions in the equity market through improved price discovery mechanism.
- Putting in place an appropriate regulatory framework.
- Reducing the transaction costs.
- Reducing information asymmetry, thereby boosting the investor confidence.

These measures were expected to increase the role of the equity market in resource mobilisation by enhancing the access of corporate sector to large resources through a variety of marketable securities. Institutional development was at the core of the reform process.

Reforms in the capital market have had a multi-dimensional impact. The significance of the capital market has improved in providing a mechanism for allocation of resources as is reflected in increase in its share in the sources of finance for the corporates. Various indicators such as reduced volatility are pointers in the direction of increase in the safety of the market. The safety of the market has also been considerably enhanced by adoption of risk management practices and the setting up of settlement guarantee funds and investor protection funds. The integrity and transparency of the market has also gone up with the wider availability of information regarding the performance of corporates. The trading and settlement framework in the Indian stock exchanges now compares favourably with the best international practices. Liquidity in the market has improved considerably.

5.1 Trading Infrastructure in Stock Exchanges

There are 23 recognised stock exchanges in India, including the Over the Counter Exchange of India (OTCEI) for small and new companies, the old established Bombay Stock Exchange (BSE) and the newer National Stock Exchange (NSE) that was set up as a model exchange to provide nation-wide services to investors. The Bombay Stock Exchange (BSE) was set up in 1875 as 'The Native Share and Stock Brokers Association'.

Equity trading is most active in the two major competing stock exchanges, viz. NSE and the BSE. Trading infrastructure in the stock exchanges is anonymous and order-driven, with all orders from market participants being matched based on strike price/time priority. As at end-May 2013, 5,230 companies were listed on the BSE, which is the largest exchange in the country. The number of listed companies in NSE as on June 30, 2013 was 1,633 which are not exclusive of BSE.

The Indian capital market is significant in terms of its degree of development, its volume of trading and of the quality of its automated trading and settlement. The capital markets—though they have suffered from periodic scandals and problems in the past—look much closer in quality to those of developed markets than those in the majority of emerging markets. The range and quality of available securities is evidenced by the substantial flows of foreign institutional investors.

The competition between NSE and BSE is a unique one by international standards, where both exchanges are in the same city and have the same trading hours. All major stocks trade on both exchanges, so the exchanges compete for order flow, and not just listings. The rise of NSE has proved to be a powerful spur to reforms at the BSE. Months after NSE started operations, the BSE also launched electronic trading, and improved rules governing admission of corporate and foreign brokerage firms. Presently, the BSE also uses an open electronic limit order book market, using satellite communications to reach locations outside Bombay.

BSE—one of the oldest exchanges in the world—accounts for the largest number of listed companies and has also started a screen-based trading system with the introduction of the Bombay On-Line Trading system. NSE—which in the recent past has accounted for the largest trading volumes—has a fully automated screen-based system that operates in the wholesale debt market segment as well as the capital market segment. BSE and NSE account for the large majority of trading volumes owing to establishment of screen-based trading and terminals in all major and many minor cities. Presently, small regional exchanges are virtually moribund.

Associated with the NSE are the National Securities Depositary Ltd. (NSDL) and the National Securities Clearing Corporation Ltd (NSCCL). The NSDL acts as the registrar for what are now predominantly dematerialized securities and the NSCCL as a clearing house.

The setting up of the NSE as an electronic trading platform set a benchmark of operating efficiency for other stock exchanges in the country. The establishment of NSDL in 1996 and Central Depository Services (India) Ltd. (CSDL) in 1999 has enabled paperless trading in the exchanges. This has also facilitated instantaneous electronic transfer of securities and eliminated the risks to the investors arising from bad deliveries in the market, delays in share transfer, fake and forged shares and loss of scrips. The electronic fund transfer (EFT) facility combined with dematerialisation of shares has created a conducive environment for reducing the settlement cycle in stock markets.

5.2 Corporatisation and Demutualisation of Stock Exchanges

Stock exchanges all over the world have been traditionally formed as *mutual* organisations. The trading members not only provide broking services, but also own, control and manage such exchanges for their mutual benefit. In India, NSE was set up as a demutualised corporate body, where ownership, management and trading rights are in the hands of three different sets of groups from its inception. The Stock Exchange, Mumbai—one of the two premier exchanges in the country—has since been corporatised and demutualised and renamed as the Bombay Stock Exchange Ltd. (BSE).

Corporate governance has emerged as an important tool for protection of shareholders. The corporate governance framework in India has evolved over a period of time since the setting up of the Kumar Mangalam Birla Committee by SEBI. According to the Economic Intelligence Unit Survey of corporate governance across the countries (2003), India was rated the third best country to have good corporate governance code after Singapore and Hong Kong. India has a reasonably well-designed regulatory framework for the issuance and trading of securities, and disclosures by the issuers with strong focus on corporate governance standards.

To enhance the level of continuous disclosure by the listed companies, SEBI amended the listing agreement to incorporate segment reporting, related party disclosures, consolidated financial results and consolidated financial statements. The listing agreement between the stock exchanges and the companies has been strengthened from time to time to enhance corporate governance standards.

5.3 Depository System, Dematerialisation (Demat) and Rematerialisation

5.3.1 Depository System: Shares are traditionally held in physical (paper) form. This method has weaknesses like loss/theft of certificates, forged/fake certificates, cumbersome and time consuming procedure for transfer of shares etc. To eliminate these weaknesses, a new system called depository system has been established. A depository is a system which holds shares of an investor in the form of electronic accounts in the same way a bank holds money of a depositor in a savings account.

A depository holds securities in dematerialised form. It maintains ownership records of securities in a book entry form and also effects transfer of ownership through book entry.

Depository system provides the following advantages to an investor:

- Shares cannot be lost, stolen or mutilated.
- An investor never needs to doubt the genuineness of his shares i.e. whether they are forged or fake.
- Share transactions like transfer, transmission etc. can be effected immediately.
- Transaction costs are usually lower than on the physical segment.
- There is no risk of bad delivery.
- Bonus/rights shares allotted to an investor will be immediately credited to his account.
- An investor receives the statement of accounts of his transactions/holdings periodically.

SEBI has introduced some degree of compulsion in trading and settlement of securities in demat form while the investors have a right to hold securities in either physical or demat form, SEBI has mandated compulsory trading and settlement of securities in select securities in dematerialised form. This was initially introduced for institutional investors and was later extended to all investors.

5.3.2 Dematerialisation (Demat): The concept of demat was introduced in Indian capital market in 1996 with the setting up of NSDL. Demat is the process by which the physical certificates of an investor are converted to an equivalent number of securities in electronic form and credited in the investor's account with his depository participant (DP).

When an investor decides to have his shares in electronic form, he should approach a depository participant (DP)—who is an agent of the depository—and open an account. He should then request for the dematerialisation of certificates by filling up a dematerialisation request form (DRF), which is available with the DP and submitting the same along with the physical certificates.

The investor has to ensure that before the certificates are handed over to the DP for demat, they are defaced by marking *Surrendered for Dematerialisation* on the face of the certificates. Before defacing the share certificate, the investor must ensure that it is available for dematerialisation. The investor must therefore check with his depository participant (DP) whether the ISIN (code number for the security in a depository system) has been activated and made available for dematerialisation by the depository. If yes, then the investor may deface the share certificate. Only those certificates can be dematerialised that are already registered in the investor's name and are in the list of securities admitted for dematerialization by National Securities Depository Limited (NSDL).

His DP will arrange to get them sent to and verified by the company, and on confirmation credit his account with an equivalent number of shares. This process is known as dematerialisation (demat). An investor can always reverse this process if he so desires and get his shares reconverted into paper format. This process is known as rematerialisation.

Benefits of demat are the following:

- Elimination of bad deliveries;
- Elimination of all risks associated with physical certification;
- No stamp duty;
- Immediate transfer and registration of securities;
- Faster settlement cycle;
- Faster disbursement of rights, bonus etc.;
- Reduction in brokerage by many brokers for trading in dematerialised securities;
- Reduction in handling of huge volumes of paper and postal delays; and
- Periodic status report.

- Elimination of problems relating to change of address of investor, transmission etc.
- Elimination of problems related to selling securities on behalf of a minor.
- Ease in portfolio monitoring.

5.3.3 Rematerialisation: If the investor wishes to get back his securities in physical form, all he has to do is to request his DP for rematerialisation of the same. Rematerialisation is the term used for converting electronic holdings back into certificates. An investor's DP will forward his request to NSDL, after verifying that he has the necessary balance. NSDL in turn will intimate the registrar who will print the certificates and dispatch the same to the investor.

5.4 Introduction of Free Pricing

Raising of capital from the securities market before 1992 was regulated under the Capital Issues (Control) Act, 1947. Firms were required to obtain approval from the Controller of Capital Issues (CCI) for raising resources in the market. New companies were allowed to issue shares only at par. Only the existing companies with substantial reserves could issue shares at a premium, which was based on some prescribed formula. In 1992, the Capital Issues (Control) Act, 1947 was repealed and with this ended all controls related to raising of resources from the market. Since then the issuers of securities can raise capital from the market without requiring any consent from any authority, either for making the issue or for pricing it. Restrictions on rights and bonus issues have also been removed. New as well as established companies are now able to price their issues according to their assessment of market conditions.

However, issuers of capital are required to meet the guidelines of SEBI on disclosure and investor protection. Companies issuing capital are required to make sufficient disclosures, including justification of the issue price and also material disclosure about the risk factors in their offer prospectus. These guidelines have served as an important measure for protecting the interest of investors and promoting the development of primary market along sound lines.

It may be recalled that in the early 1990s, the liberalisation of the industrial sector and free pricing of capital issues led to an increased number of companies tapping the primary capital market to mobilise resources. Several corporates charged a high premium not justified by their fundamentals. Also, several companies vanished after raising resources from the capital market. SEBI, therefore, strengthened the norms for public issues while retaining the freedom of the issuers to enter the new issues market and to freely price their issues. The disclosure standards were also strengthened for companies coming out with public issues for improving the levels of investor protection.

Strict disclosure norms and entry point restrictions prescribed by SEBI made it difficult for most new companies without an established track record to access the public issues market. Whereas this helped to improve the quality of paper coming into the market, it contributed to a decline in the number of issues and the amount mobilised from the market.

5.5 Strengthening of Disclosure Norms

The central goal of securities markets is to obtain a widely-dispersed ownership and trading in securities. There is conflict of interest between the management team, which controls the firm, and the shareholders, who run the firm. Many policy efforts in recent years have been devoted towards improving incentives to managers to maximise the interests of shareholders.

Improvements in disclosure are a central tool for containing the conflicts of interest between the managers and shareholders. In order to foster improvements in disclosure, SEBI set up a system named Electronic Data Information Filing and Retrieval (EDIFAR) in July 2002. This system offers a mechanism through which firms would electronically file mandatory disclosures to SEBI, and these documents would be available to individuals over the internet, with a near-zero delay. It is envisaged that in the future, disclosure would take place through company websites, exchange websites, and EDIFAR.

For strengthening the process of information flow from the listed companies, several measures have been introduced: (a) while sufficient disclosures are mandatory for the companies at the stage of public issues, the listed companies are also required under the listing agreement to make disclosures on a continued basis, (b) for ensuring quick flow of information to the public, the decision pertaining to dividend, bonus and right announcements or any material event are now required to be disclosed to the public within 15 minutes of the conclusion of the board meeting in which the disclosures are taken, and (c) accounting practices were streamlined with norms introduced for segment reporting, related to party transactions and consolidated balance sheets.

There is a substantial scale of securities issuance taking place through the private placement route. The private placement route has become a mechanism where securities can be placed with a few wholesale buyers of securities, without incurring the overheads of the public issue. SEBI is working on devising clear institutional mechanisms through which some public disclosure is made about these issues, while preserving the rights of issuers to not use the public issue route if it is considered to involve excessive overhead costs.

Without seeking to control the freedom of the issuers to enter the market and freely price their issues, the norms for public issues were made stringent in April 1996 to prevent fraudulent companies from accessing the market. Issuers of capital are now required to disclose information on various aspects such as track record of profitability, risk factors etc.

As a result, there has been an improvement in the standards of disclosure in the offer documents for the public and rights issues and easier accessibility of information to the investors. The improvement in disclosure standards has enhanced transparency, thereby improving the level of investor protection.

5.6 Transparency and Efficiency

The National Stock Exchange (NSE) introduced screen-based trading at its inception in 1992 which was followed by other stock exchanges. Screen-based trading makes on-line, electronic, anonymous and order-driven transactions possible. It is a transparent system which provides equal access to all investors, irrespective of their geographical locations.

The move to an electronic trading system has resulted in transparency in trades, better price discovery and lower transaction costs. The efficiency of the market has improved through faster execution of trades. The operational efficiency of the stock market has also been strengthened through improvements in the clearing and settlement practices and the risk management process. Almost the entire delivery of securities now takes place in dematerialised form. Over the past few years or so, there has been no instance of postponement or clubbing of settlements at two main stock exchanges (BSE and NSE) despite defaults by brokers. The cases of bad deliveries are close to nil. Insider trading has been made a criminal offence. Non-transparent products like *badla* have been banned.

The setting up of trade/settlement guarantee funds in most of the exchanges has considerably reduced settlement risks for investors. Corporate governance practices and disclosure norms have led to transparency in information flows, which in turn have improved the price discovery process.

In order to bring greater transparency to the debt market, and to move away from bilateral negotiation towards anonymous order-matching, trading in government bonds began on stock exchanges on January 16, 2003. This has involved exploiting the identical process flow used for trading in equities. Trade takes place by anonymous order matching for all orders across the country, risk management is done by the clearing corporation, and settlement takes place at the depository. Under this system, government bonds appear in the depository statement of an investor alongside corporate equities and bonds. This system has several strengths.

- Anonymous trading avoids the supervisory and regulatory difficulties of the telephone market, where counterparties are aware of identities and can engage in trades at off-market prices.
- This market design offers symmetric market access from locations all over India and over the internet, as opposed to the telephone market, which favours entities in south Bombay.
- It exploits information technology to guarantees that orders are matched against the best price available in the country. This is in contrast with the telephone market, where traders can search for counterparties, but are not sure of having found the best counter party.
- It is fully transparent in that orders and trades are visible in real time. This is in contrast with the telephone market, where orders are not visible, and the transparency of trades is limited and delayed.
- It exploits the information technology of the depositories of the equity market (NSDL and CDSL), which have the full range of functionality required for investors such as a wide network of IT-enabled depository participants, internet access, strong computer security, access to data about the beneficial owner down to the end-investor.

Issuers also have the option of raising resources through fixed price mechanism or the book building process. [Book-building is a process by which demand for the securities proposed to be issued is built-up and the price for securities is assessed for determination of the quantum of such securities to be issued.] Book building was introduced to improve the transparency in pricing of the scrips and determine proper market price for shares.

5.7 Shortening of Settlement Cycle

Following the enactment of the Depository Act, 1996, two depositories were set up: Central Depository Services Ltd. (CDSL) and National Securities Depository Limited (NSDL). The CDSL and NSDL have been successful in the dematerialisation of securities almost to the full extent. Presently, the transfer of ownership is mostly done through book-entry form. This has greatly improved the speed, accuracy and security of the settlement system. Prior to these arrangements, the settlement cycle was as high as 14 days for specified scrips and 30 days for others. The settlement risk was very high because of unforeseen happenings between the transaction and the settlement. To begin with, the settlement cycle was reduced to a week. Thereafter, rolling settlement was introduced on a T+5 basis in July 2001. From December 2001, all scrips which had established connectivity with the above-mentioned Depositories were moved to rolling settlement. The settlement cycle was further reduced to T+3 in April 2002 and to T+2 in April 2003.

5.8 Growth of Service Providers

Besides strengthening the institutional design of the markets, the reforms have also brought about an increase in the number of service providers who add value to the market. The most significant development in this respect has been the setting up of credit rating agencies. By assigning ratings to debt instruments and by continuous monitoring and dissemination of the ratings, they help in improving the quality of information. At present, four credit rating agencies are operating in India. Besides, two other service providers, *viz.* registrars to issue and share transfer agents, have also grown in number, which help in spreading the services easily and at competitive prices.

5.9 Protection of Investors

The stock exchanges have put in place a system for

redressal of investor grievances for matters relating to trading members and companies. They ensure that critical and price-sensitive information reaching the exchange is made available to all classes of investor at the same point of time. Further, to protect the interests of investors, the Investor Protection Fund (IPF) has also been set up by the stock exchanges. The exchanges maintain an IPF to take care of investor claims, which may arise out of non-settlement of obligations by the trading member, who has been declared a defaulter, in respect of trades executed on the exchange. Measures of investor protection that have been put in place over the reform period have led to increased confidence among investors. To improve the availability of information to investors, all listed companies are required to publish unaudited financial results on a quarterly basis.

A continuing increase in the savings rate of households suggests that there is no supply constraint in terms of financial resources that could be channelled into the equity market. After the exuberance of the stock market in the mid-1990s and its decline thereafter, a large number of individual investors took flight to safety in bank deposits, safe retirement instruments and insurance. Households in India have increasingly tended to prefer savings in the form of safe and contractual instruments as opposed to capital market based instruments. Although retail investors have started showing some increased interest in the equity market in recent years, there is a need to increase their participation further.

5.10 Portfolio Investment Flows

Since early 1990s there has been enhanced flow of cross-border portfolio investments, especially by foreign institutional investors (FIIs), from developed countries to the developing countries. Portfolio investors provide institutional character to the capital markets, flavoured by highly intensive research and diversified investments. FII investments inject global liquidity into the markets, raise the price-earning ratio and thus reduce the cost of capital.

FIIs make investments in various countries to provide a measure of portfolio diversification and hedging to their assets. The forces driving the recent change in the investment portfolio of FIIs—as reflected in the growing emphasis on equities of emerging market economies—have included, *inter alia*, (a) increased accessibility of these markets after liberalisation, (b) improved marketability, (c) fewer problems relating to thin trading, and (d) improved macroeconomic fundamentals of these countries.

Merits of FII flows apart, the Mexican crisis and the East Asian crisis highlighted the downside risks of such flows. The downside risks include political risk, currency risk, problems associated with low liquidity and volatility on returns. Reversal of portfolio flows can be disorderly and result in substantial economic hardship for developing countries.

The main problem in managing portfolio flows towards developing countries emanates from the larger volatility associated with such flows as compared to FDI. It has been argued that under the process of globalisation, highly diversified investors participate in cross-border movement of capital.

Such investors pay little attention to economic fundamentals and in the presence of asymmetric information they resort to herd behaviour, which results in volatility of international capital flows. Such a view has, however, been challenged and it has been argued that there is high level of substitutability between various forms of foreign capital.

Economies with modest growth potentials and semi-developed financial market infrastructure are most vulnerable to reversal of portfolio investment flows. Existence of large asymmetry of information among the domestic companies and foreign investors in such countries can lead to sharp changes in portfolio and private debt flows in the face of even a slight change in investor perception about the health of the recipient economy or its financial system. This type of volatility is, however, not limited to portfolio flows. Even external commercial borrowings, in the form of bank borrowing or bond financing, show similar pattern.

FII investments first started flowing to India in 1993. Portfolio investment inflows have since then been substantial. ADR/GDR issues by Indian companies are another important source of cross-border portfolio investment in India. Volatility of cross-border portfolio investment flows into India has been less than what has been experienced by other emerging market economies (EMEs). The stability in portfolio flows to India has been attributed to factors such as robust economic performance since early 1990s and relatively low level of co-movements between Indian and global stock prices.

Prior to 1992, only non-resident Indians (NRIs) and overseas corporate bodies (OCBs) were allowed to undertake portfolio investment in India. In line with the recommendations of the High Level Committee on Balance of Payments (Chairman: C. Rangarajan), 1993, FIIs were allowed to invest in the Indian debt and equity market. Ceilings on FII investments have been progressively relaxed, and at present aggregate investment by FIIs in a company is allowed within the sectoral cap prescribed for FDI. Apart from equity, FIIs registered under the 100 percent debt route can invest in debt instruments—both Government as well as corporate, the current aggregate ceiling being US$ 1 billion.

Indian corporates are also allowed to access equity capital from foreign sources in the form of ADR/GDR and Euro issues. Policies on international offerings on ADRs/GDRs have been liberalised substantially and corporates are allowed to raise funds by way of ADRs/GDRs under an automatic route, subject to specified guidelines.

Two-way fungibility in ADR/GDR issues of Indian companies has been introduced under which investors in India can purchase shares and deposit them with an Indian custodian for issue of ADRs/GDRs by the overseas depository to the extent of the ADRs/GDRs converted into underlying shares.

A major issue which will influence India's securities markets in the future is the challenge of globalisation. RBI has increasingly moved in the direction of giving access to international diversification to institutional investors and individual investors in India. Financial intermediaries and exchanges in India will also experience global competition. There is a need for fully integrating a global perspective into the plans of firms, exchanges, regulators and policy makers.

6

Capital Market Instruments

Capital market instruments fall into two broad groups: (i) direct instruments, and (ii) derivates instruments. Direct instruments include the following:

1. Ordinary (or equity) shares.
2. Preference shares.
3. Debentures.

While the ordinary and preference shares represent ownership instruments, debentures and innovating debt instruments are creditorship securities.

6.1 Ordinary Shares

Ordinary shares represent ownership capital and their owners—ordinary shareholders—share the reward and risk associated with ownership of corporate enterprises. They are called ordinary shares in contrast with preference shares which carry certain prior rights with regard to income and redemption.

There are certain concepts associated with ordinary shares. Authorised equity represents the maximum amount that a company can raise from the ordinary shareholders. It can be changed in the prescribed manner. The portion of the authorized capital offered by the company to investors is the issued capital. Subscribed share capital is that part of the issued capital which has been subscribed by the investors. The actual amount paid by the shareholders is the paid-up capital. The issued, subscribed and paid-up capitals are generally the same.

Ordinary shares typically have a face value in terms of the price of each share, the most popular denomination being ₹ 10. However, companies are permitted to issue such shares without a face value. The price at which the ordinary shares are issued is the issue price. The issue price for new companies is generally equal to the face value. It may be higher for existing companies, the difference being the share premium. The book value of ordinary shares refers to the paid-up capital plus reserves and surplus (net worth) divided by the number of outstanding shares. The price at which ordinary shares are traded in the stock market is their market value.

Ordinary shares have some special features in terms of the rights and claims of their holders: (a) residual claim to income/assets, (b) right to control, (c) pre-emptive rights, and (d) limited liability.

Ordinary shareholders have a residual claim to the income of the company. They are entitled to the remaining income/profits of the company after all outside claims are met. The amount actually received by the shareholders in the form of dividend depends on the decision of the Board of Directors. The directors have the right to decide what portion of the earning will be distributed to the shareholders as cash dividend and what portion will be ploughed back as retained earnings, which the shareholders may receive later in the form of capital appreciation/bonus shares.

The ordinary shareholders' claim in the assets of the company is also residual in that their claim would rank after the claims of the creditors and preference shareholders in the event of liquidation. If the liquidation value of assets is insufficient, their claims may remain unpaid.

As owners of the company, ordinary shareholders have the right to control the operations of, participate in the management of, the company. Their control is, however, indirect. The major policies/decisions are approved by the board of directors and the board-appointed management carries out the day-to-day operations. The shareholders have the legal right/power to elect the board of directors as well as vote on every resolution placed in various meetings of the company.

The ordinary shareholders exercise their right to control the company through voting in the meetings of the company. According to the most commonly used system of voting in India, namely majority rule voting, each share carries one vote. As a result, shareholders/groups holding more than 50 percent of the outstanding equity shares are able to elect all the directors of their choice.

The ordinary shareholders of a company enjoy pre-emptive rights in the sense that they have a legal right to be offered, by the company, the first opportunity to purchase additional issues of equity capital in proportion to their existing holdings.

Although ordinary shareholders share the ownership risk, their liability is limited to the extent of their investment in the share capital of the company.

6.2 Preference Shares

Preference shares are a unique type of long-term capital market instruments in that they combine some of the features of ordinary shares as well as some features of debentures. Thus,

- As a hybrid form of financial instrument, they are similar to debentures insofar as they carry a fixed rate of dividend.
- They rank higher than ordinary shares as claimants to the income/assets of the company.
- Generally, preference shareholders do not have voting rights.
- They do not have a share in residual earnings/assets.
- Dividend on preference shares is paid out of divisible/after tax profit.
- Payment of preference dividend depends on the discretion of the management, i.e. it is not an obligatory payment and non-payment does not force insolvency/liquidation.
- Irredeemable types of preference shares have no fixed maturity date.

Preference shares have a prior claim over ordinary shares

both on the income and assets of the company. In other words, preference dividend must be paid in full before payment of any dividend on ordinary shares. In the event of liquidation, the whole of preference share capital must be paid before anything is paid to the ordinary shareholders. Thus, preference shares stand midway between debentures and ordinary shares as regards claims on the income and assets of the company. Stated in terms of risk perspective, preference shares are less risky than ordinary shares but more risky than debentures.

6.3 Debentures

Debentures represent creditorship securities and debentures holders are long-term creditors of the company. As a secured instrument, it is a promise to pay interest and repay principal at stipulated times.

The payment of interest and repayment of principal is a contractual obligation enforceable by law. Failure/default leads to bankruptcy of the company. The claim of debenture holders on income and assets ranks pari passu with other secured debt and higher than that of shareholders—preference as well as ordinary shares.

Convertible debentures give the holders the right (option) to convert them into equity shares on certain terms. They are entitled to a fixed income till the conversion option is exercised and share the benefits associated with equity shares after the conversion.

6.4 Types of Orders

In the stock market, when prices of the well-traded securities are quoted, full prices are seldom indicated. The various kinds of order given by various traders are explained below:

6.4.1 Market Order: Market order is the most common type of order and simply involves an instruction to buy or sell at the prevailing price in the market. It represents the best price one can get at a point of time. Small orders can be conveniently executed at the market rate but if the size of the order is larger than the volume which is currently available in the dealing pit, then executions might not all be at the same price because the dealer would have to bid up or offer down until desired volumes are secured. Thus, large orders *at market* have a tendency to move against those who give them. No wonder then that large orders may be placed by market participants who wish to move the market in a particular direction.

6.4.2 Limit Order: A limit order is an order to buy or sell at a specified price, or a price better than that. Thus, a limit order is exemplified when a client may give a broker a price limit above which he should not buy or below which he should not sell. Also, there is a time limit for which it may be given. This kind of an order puts more responsibility on the dealer since he has to be aware of his limits orders once the limit is reached. A limit order kind of order is feasible when it is considered that there is sufficient market force in the opposite direction at current prices. This has the advantage that it is far less likely to push prices in an adverse direction.

6.4.3 Stop-Loss Order: A stop-loss order is aimed at closing out positions when a particular price level is traded. It is this kind of an order when a client orders his broker to sell a share or some other security, if its market price falls to a certain level below the current price. Thus, once the specified price is reached or penetrated, the order becomes the market order. Stop-loss orders are a good means of protecting profits or limiting losses while waiting for the market to recover.

6.4.4 Stop-Limit Order: A stop-limit order is said to be placed when, for example, a client can place a stop order at a particular level with a limit beyond which the market would cease to be chased.

6.4.5 Fill or Kill Order: This is an order to a broker to buy or sell a security or derivative immediately. If the order is not executed at once, it is treated as withdrawn. This type of an order is often used by a party wishing to take out a large bid/offer but, in case of a failure, it does not wish to be viewed as a possible large counter party in the market.

6.4.6 Market if Touched (MIT): It is a limit order which automatically becomes a market order once a predetermined price is reached.

6.4.7 Good Till Cancelled (GTC): This is a client's order to buy or sell, usually at a specified price, which remains valid until its execution or cancellation.

6.4.8 Day Order or Good for the Day: As the name implies, this means the limits or stop order would lapse at the end of the day (of dealing) if it has not been executed during the day.

6.5 Financial Derivatives

6.5.1 Emergence of Complex Financial Products: In recent years, complex financial products such as asset-backed securities, derivatives, credit-default swaps (CDSs) and collateralised debt obligations (CDOs) have proliferated in developed countries. These products have become highly popular with banks and financial institutions as they allow them to hedge their risks and manage their regulatory and economic capital more efficiently.

Although various structured products have enabled the transfer of risks and enhanced the liquidity of instruments, the recent turmoil in the US sub-prime mortgage market and related developments connected with complex derivatives have also brought to the fore the risks posed by these instruments.

The emergence of the market for derivative products, most notably forwards, futures and options, can be traced back to the willingness of risk-averse economic agents to guard themselves against uncertainties arising out of fluctuations in asset prices. By their very nature, the financial markets are marked by a very high degree of volatility. Through the use of derivative products, it is possible to partially or fully transfer price risks by locking-in asset prices. As instruments of risk management, derivatives generally do not influence the fluctuations in the underlying asset prices. However, by locking-in asset prices, derivative products minimize the impact of fluctuations in asset prices on the profitability and cash flow situation of risk-averse investors.

Derivative products initially emerged as hedging devices against fluctuations in commodity prices and commodity-linked derivatives remained the sole form of such products for a long time. The financial derivatives came into spotlight in post-1970 period due to growing instability in the financial markets. However, since their emergence, financial derivatives have become very popular and by 1990s, they accounted for about two-thirds of total transactions in derivative products. In recent years, the market for financial derivatives has grown tremendously both in terms of variety of instruments available, their complexity and also turnover.

In India also financial products such as mortgage-backed securities (MBS) and asset-backed securities (ABS) are in existence. Besides the securitised products, the Indian forex and rupee derivative markets have also developed significantly over the years.

In respect of forex derivatives involving rupee, residents have access to foreign exchange forward contracts, foreign currency-rupee swap instruments and currency options--both cross currency and foreign currency-rupee. As stated in the Annual Policy Statement for the year 2008-09, the Reserve Bank of India (RBI) announced the introduction of currency futures in the eligible exchanges for which the broad framework was announced in August 2008. In future, some more innovative and complex products might emerge. These products may pose several regulatory and supervisory challenges.

6.5.2 Meaning of Derivatives: Derivative in mathematics means a variable derived from another variable. The term *derivative* indicates that it has no independent value, i.e. its value is entirely *derived* from the value of the underlying asset. The underlying asset can be security, commodity, bullion, currency, live stock or anything else. In other words, derivative means a forward, future, option or any other hybrid contract of pre-determined fixed duration, linked for the purpose of contract fulfilment to the value of a specified real or financial asset of an index of securities. Similarly, in the financial sense, a derivative is a financial product, which has been derived from a market for another product. Without the underlying product, derivatives do not have any independent existence in the market.

Derivative instruments are defined by the Indian Securities Contracts (Regulation) Act, 1956 to include: (i) a security derived from a debt instrument, share, secured/unsecured loan, risk instrument or contract for differences, or any other form of security, and (ii) a contract that derives its value from the prices/index of prices of underlying securities.

In other words, derivatives are financial instruments and/or contracts whose value depends upon the value of an underlying. Since their value is essentially derived out of an underlying, they are financial abstractions whose value is derived mathematically from the changes in the value of the underlying.

The International Monetary Fund (IMF) defines derivatives as "financial instruments that are linked to a specific financial instrument or indicator or commodity and through which specific financial risks can be traded in financial markets in their own right. The value of a financial derivative derives from the price of an underlying item, such as an asset or index. Unlike debt securities, no principal is advanced to be repaid and no investment income accrues".

Derivatives have come into being because of the existence of risks in business. Thus, derivatives are means of managing risks. The parties managing risks in the market are known as *hedgers*. Some people/organizations are in the business of taking risks to earn profits. Such entities represent the *speculators*. The third players in the market, known as the *arbitragers,* take advantage of the market mistakes.

In recent years, derivatives have become increasingly important in the field of finance. While futures and options are now actively traded on many exchanges, forward contracts are popular on the over-the-counter (OTC) market.

6.5.3 Reasons for the Popularity of Derivatives: Financial derivatives have become popular due to the following reasons:

- Increased volatility in asset prices in financial markets.
- Increased integration of national financial markets with the international markets.
- Marked improvement in communication facilities and sharp decline in their costs.
- Development of more sophisticated risk management tools, providing economic agents a wider choice of risk management strategies.
- Innovations in the derivatives markets, which optimally combine the risks and returns over a large number of financial assets, leading to higher returns, reduced risk as well as transaction costs as compared to individual financial assets.

In the class of equity derivatives, futures and options on stock indices have gained more popularity than on individual stocks, especially among institutional investors, who are major users of index-linked derivatives. Even small investors find these useful due to high correlation of the popular indices with various portfolios and ease of use. The lower costs associated with index derivatives vis-à-vis derivative products based on individual securities is another reason for their growing use.

6.6 Variants (or Types) of Derivative Contracts

Derivative contracts have several variants. The most common variants are forwards, futures, options and swaps.

6.6.1 Forwards/Forward Contracts: A forward contract is a customised contract between two entities, where settlement takes place on a specific date in the future at today's pre-agreed price. A forward contract is an agreement to buy or sell an asset on a specified date for specified price. One of the parties to the contract assumes a long position and agrees to buy the underlying asset on a certain specified future date, for a certain specified price. The other party assumes a short position and agrees to sell the asset on the same date for the same price. Other contract details like delivery date, price and quantity are negotiated bilaterally by the parties to the contract. Forward contracts are normally traded outside stock exchanges. They are popular on the Over the Counter (OTC) market.

The salient features of forward contracts are as follows:

- They are bilateral contracts and hence exposed to counter party risk.
- Each contract is customer designed, and, hence, is unique in terms of contract size, expiration date and the asset type and quality.
- The contract price is generally not available in public domain.
- On the expiration date, the contract has to be settled by delivery for the asset.
- If a party wishes to reverse the contract, it has to compulsorily go to the same counterparty, which often results in a high price being charged.

Forward contracts are very useful in hedging and speculation. A typical hedging application may pertain to an exporter who expects to receive payment in US dollars, 2 months later. He is exposed to the risk of exchange rate fluctuations. By using the currency forward market to sell dollars forward, he can lock-on a rate today and reduce his uncertainty. Likewise, an importer who is required to make a payment in US dollars 2 months hence can reduce his exposure to exchange rate fluctuations by buying dollars forward.

6.6.2 Futures/Future Contracts: Future contracts are special types of forward contracts in the sense that the former are standardised exchange-traded contracts. Future contract markets are designed to solve the problems that exist in forward markets. A future contract is an agreement between two parties to buy or sell an asset at a certain time in future, at a certain price. However, unlike forward contracts, future contracts are standardized and stock exchange-traded. To facilitate liquidity in the future contracts, the exchange specifies certain standard features for the contract. It is a standardized contract with a standard underlying instrument, a standard quantity and quality of the underlying instrument that can be delivered, and a standard timing of such settlement. A future contract may be offset prior to maturity by entering into an equal and opposite transaction. The standardized items in a future contract are the following:

1. Quantity of the underlying.
2. Quality of the underlying.
3. Date/month of delivery.
4. Units of price quotation and minimum price change.
5. Location of settlement.

6.6.3 Options: Options are fundamentally different from forward and future contracts. An option gives the holder of the option the right to do something. The holder does not have to necessarily exercise this right. In contrast, in a forward or future contract, the two parties commit themselves to doing something. Whereas it costs nothing (except margin requirements) to enter into a future contract, the purchase of an option requires an up front payment.

Options are of two types: calls options and put options. Calls options give the buyer the right but not the obligation to buy a given quantity of the underlying asset, at a given price on or before a given future date. Put options give the buyer the right, but not the obligation to sell a given quantity of the underlying asset at a given price on or before a given date.

A. Warrants: Options generally have lives of up to 1 year, the majority of options traded on options exchanges having maximum maturity of 9 months. Longer-dated options are called *warrants* and are generally traded over-the-counter.

B. LEAPS: The acronym LEAPS means Long-term

Equity Anticipation Securities. These are options having a maturity of up to 3 years.

C. Baskets: Basket options are options on portfolios of underlying assets. The underlying asset is usually a moving average or a basket of assets. Equity index options are a form of basket options.

6.6.4 Swaps: Swaps are private agreements between two parties to exchange cash flows in the future according to a pre-arranged formula. They can be regarded as portfolios of forward contracts. Following are the two commonly used swaps:

A. Interest Rate Swaps: These entail swapping of only the interest-related cash flows between the parties in the same currency.

B. Currency Swaps: These entail swapping of both principal and interest between the parties, with the cash flows in one direction being in a different currency than those in the opposite direction.

6.6.5 Swaptions: Swaptions are options to buy or sell a swap that will become operative at the expiry of the options. Thus, swaption is an option on a forward swap. Rather than have call options and put options, the swaptions market has receiver swaptions and payer swaptions.

6.7 Participants in the Derivatives Market

The following three broad categories of participants, viz. hedgers, speculators, and arbitrageurs trade in the derivatives market.

6.7.1 Hedgers: Hedgers face risk associated with the price of an asset. They use future or option markets to reduce or eliminate this risk. In other words, hedgers are those who wish to protect their existing exposures and essentially are safety-driven.

6.7.2 Speculators: They bet on future movements in the price of an asset. Future and option contracts can give them an extra leverage; that is, they can increase both the potential gains and potential losses in a speculative venture. Speculators are willing risk takers who are expectation-driven.

6.7.3 Arbitrageurs: They are in business to take advantage of a discrepancy between prices in two different markets. If, for example, they see the futures price of an asset getting out of line with the cash price, they will take offsetting positions in the two markets to lock-in a profit. Arbitragers are traders and market-makers who deal in buying and selling derivatives contracts hoping to profit from price-differentials between different markets. A market maker is one who provides two-way quotes for a given product and thereby runs a position in that product.

6.8 Economic Role of Derivatives

Derivative markets perform three essential economic functions:

1. Risk management.
2. Price discovery.
3. Transactional efficiency.

The first function refers to the ability of traders to offset financial risks through derivatives. The principal benefit of the derivatives market is that it provides the opportunity for risk management through hedging. Derivatives are innovations in risk management not in risk itself.

The second refers to the better allocation of resources in an economy that is created by the wide availability of an equilibrium price which serves as a measure of value.

The third function alludes to increased efficiency of transacting through derivatives. Derivative markets reduce the costs of trading and raising capital, thereby enhancing their risk management and price discovery functions.

Derivatives have played a major role in the development of financial markets and their integration across several economies, especially in developed countries. Derivatives serve to achieve a more complete financial system because previously fixed combinations of the risk properties of loans and financial assets can be bundled and unbundled into new synthetic assets. For instance, structured products or synthetic derivatives could be created by adding elementary assets or underlying assets such as bonds, equities and borrowing and lending instruments with a combination of derivative products such as put and call options. Repackaging risk properties in this way can provide a more perfect match between an investor's risk preferences and the effective risk of the portfolio or cash-flow. Derivatives allow individual risk elements of an asset to be priced and traded individually, thus ensuring an efficient price system in the asset markets.

The economic functions performed by derivatives market can be summarised as under:

- Derivatives market helps to increase savings and investment in the long-run. Transfer of risk enables market participants to expand their volume of activity.
- Derivatives trading acts as a catalyst for new entrepreneurial activity. Derivatives have a history of attracting many bright, creative, well educated people with an entrepreneurial attitude.
- Prices in an organized derivatives market reflect the perception of the market participants about the future and lead the prices of underlying to the perceived future level.
- Prices of derivatives converge with the prices of the underlying at the expiration of the derivatives contract. In fact, derivatives help in the discovery of the future as well as current prices.
- Derivatives market helps to transfer risks from those who have them but may not like them to those who have an appetite for them.
- Derivatives, due to their inherent nature are linked to the underlying cash markets. With the introduction of derivatives, the underlying market witnesses higher trading volumes because of participation by more players who would not otherwise participate for lack of an arrangement to transfer risk.

- Speculative trades shift to a more controlled environment of derivatives market. In the absence of an organized derivatives market, speculators trade in the underlying cash markets. Margining, monitoring and surveillance of the activities of various participants become extremely difficult in these kinds of mixed markets.

6.9 L.C. Gupta Committee on Derivatives Trading in India

India has introduced different equity derivatives in a phased manner. This phased approach was adopted in India with index futures being introduced in June 2000, index options in June 2001 and individual stock options in July 2001.

Securities and Exchange Board of India (SEBI) set up a 24-member committee under the Chairmanship of L.C. Gupta on November 18, 1996 to develop appropriate regulatory framework for derivatives trading in India. The Committee submitted its report on March 17, 1998 prescribing necessary preconditions for introduction of derivatives trading in India. The committee recommended that derivatives should be declared as *securities* so that regulatory framework applicable to trading of *securities* could also govern trading of derivatives.

The Committee outlined the goals of regulation in Paragraph 3.1 of its report which is reproduced here, "The Committee believes that regulation should be designed to achieve specific, well-defined goals. It is inclined towards positive regulation designed to encourage healthy activity and behaviour. It has been guided by the following objectives:

6.9.1 Investor Protection: Attention needs to be given to the following four aspects:

- **Fairness and Transparency:** The trading rules should ensure that trading is conducted in a fair and transparent manner. Experience in other countries shows that in many cases, derivative brokers/dealers failed to disclose potential risk to the clients. In this context, sales practices adopted by dealers for derivatives would require specific regulation. In some of the most widely reported mishaps in the derivatives market elsewhere, the underlying reason was inadequate internal control system at the user-firm itself so that overall exposure was not controlled and the use of derivatives was for speculation rather than for risk hedging. These experiences provide useful lessons for us for designing regulations.

- **Safeguard for Clients' Money:** Money and securities deposited by clients with the trading members should not only be kept in a separate clients' account but should also not be attachable for meeting the broker's own debts. It should be ensured that trading by dealers on own account is totally segregated from that for clients.
- **Competent and Honest Service:** The eligibility criteria for trading members should be designed to encourage competent and qualified personnel so that investors/clients are served well. This makes it necessary to prescribe qualification for derivatives brokers/dealers and the sales persons appointed by them in terms of a knowledge base.
- **Market Integrity:** The trading system should ensure that the market's integrity is safeguarded by minimising the possibility of defaults. This requires framing appropriate rules about capital adequacy, margins, clearing corporation etc.

6.9.2 Derivative Products:

A. Interest and Currency Futures: The Committee stated in Paragraph 1.24, "There are inter-connections among the various kinds of financial futures [equity, interest rate and currency], because the various financial markets are closely inter-linked, as the recent financial market turmoil in East and South-East Asian countries has shown. The basic principles underlying the running of future markets and their regulation are the same. Having a common trading infrastructure will have important advantages. The Committee, therefore, feels that the attempt should be to develop an integrated market structure".

B. Single Stock Derivatives: The Committee advocated a phased introduction of different equity derivatives in India in Paragraph 2.17 of its report, "The consensus in the Committee was that stock index futures would be the best starting point for equity derivatives in India. The Committee has arrived at this conclusion after careful examination of all aspects of the problem, including the survey findings and regulatory preparedness. The Committee would favour the introduction of other types of equity derivatives also, as the derivatives market grows and the market players acquire familiarity with its operations. Other equity derivatives include options on stock index or on individual stocks. There may also be room for more than one stock index futures. It is bound to be a gradual process, shaped by market forces under the over-all supervision of SEBI".

The Committee was not much inclined towards the fourth type of equity derivatives (individual stock futures) given its then limited popularity globally, "The fourth type, viz. individual stock futures, was favoured much less. It is pertinent to note that the US does not permit individual stock futures. Only one or two countries in the world are known to have futures on individual stocks". (Paragraph 2.3)

6.9.3 Use of Derivatives by Mutual Funds: The Committee recommended that mutual funds should be permitted to use derivatives for hedging and portfolio rebalancing, "Mutual funds should be allowed to use financial derivatives for hedging purposes (including anticipated hedging) and portfolio re-balancing within a policy framework and rules laid down by their Board of Trustees who should specify what derivatives are allowed to be used, within what limits, for what purposes, for which schemes, and also the authorisation procedure". (Paragraph 7.10)

6.9.4 SEBI Related Issues: The Committee very rightly emphasised the need for SEBI to build competencies in the area of derivatives, "SEBI should immediately create a special Derivatives Cell because derivatives demand special knowledge. It should encourage its staff members to undergo training in derivatives and also recruit some specialised personnel.

A Derivatives Advisory Council may also be created to tap the outside expertise for independent advice on many problems which are bound to arise from time to time in regard to derivatives". [Paragraph 4.11(b)]

6.10 Amendment of Securities Contract Regulation Act

In pursuance of the recommendations of the L.C. Gupta Committee, Securities Contract Regulation Act (SCRA) was amended in December 1999 to include derivatives within the ambit of *securities* and the regulatory framework was developed for governing derivatives trading. The Act also made it clear that derivatives shall be legal and valid only if such contracts are traded on a recognised stock exchange, thus precluding OTC derivatives. The government also rescinded in March 2000, the three-decade old notification, which prohibited forward trading in securities.

Derivatives trading commenced in India in June 2000 after SEBI granted the final approval to this effect in May 2000. SEBI permitted the derivatives segments of two stock exchanges NSE and BSE, and their clearing house/corporation to commence trading and settlement in approved derivative contracts. To begin with, SEBI approved trading in index future contracts based on S&P CNX Nifty and BSE-30 (Sensex) index. This was followed by approval for trading in options which commenced in June 2001 and the trading in options on individual securities commenced in July 2001. Future contracts on individual stocks were launched in November 2001. Trading and settlement in derivative contracts is done in accordance with the rules, bylaws, and regulations of the respective exchanges and their clearing house/corporation duly approved by SEBI and notified in the official gazette.

6.11 Measures to Protect the Rights of Investors in the Derivatives Market

Investors' money has to be kept separate at all levels and is permitted to be used only against the liability of he investor and is not available to the trading member or clearing member or even any other investor.

A trading member is required to provide every investor with a risk disclosure document which will disclose the risks associated with the derivatives trading so that investors can take a conscious decision to trade in derivatives.

Investors get the contract note duly time stamped for receipt of the order and execution of the order. The order is executed with the identity of the client and without client ID order is not accepted by the system. The investors can demand the trade confirmation slip with their respective ID in support of the contract note. This protects them from the risk of price favours, if any, extended by the Member.

In the derivatives market all money paid by the investors towards margins on all open positions is kept in trust with the clearing house/clearing corporation and in the event of default of the trading or clearing member the amounts paid by the client towards margins are segregated and not utilized towards the default of the member. However, in the event of default of a member, losses suffered by the investors, if any, on settled/closed out position are compensated from the investors' protection fund, as per the rules, bylaws and regulations of the derivative segment of the exchanges.

6.12 Recent Developments in the Derivatives Market

The derivatives market got a shot in the arm with the Government deciding to treat income from derivatives trading as a non-speculative income.

The decision to treat income from derivative trading as a non-speculative income will contribute to an increase in trading volume in the derivative market since it provides for setting off of derivative income/loss against normal income/loss.

FIIs are permitted to submit appropriate collateral, in cash or otherwise when trading in domestic derivatives. According to market players, this will bring about flexibility and encourage FIIs to take greater exposure through the derivative contracts.

Local players already had the flexibility of submitting collaterals, such as bank guarantee or shares or deposit receipt, in place of cash or along with cash, for meeting their margin obligations.

7

Price Multiples: Review of Literature

7.1 Review of Literature for Matured Markets

Beaver, Lambert and Morse (1980) show how changes in price and changes in earnings are related when price is used as a proxy for extra information given to market players. This relationship provides an interpretation of the contemporaneous association between price changes and earnings changes previously observed by Ball and Brown (1968) and Beaver, Clarke and Wright (1979) among others. It also provides a basis for inferring from prices the earnings process and the expected future earnings as perceived by market participants. They use the stochastic process of accounting earnings. In this paper they infer market participants' expectations regarding future earnings from observed changes in security pries. They use price data to infer a characterization of the stochastic process generating earnings, as perceived by the market participants.

The notion that price conveys information about expectations is pervasive. In general the expected value of future earnings conditioned upon past earnings will not equal the expected value of future earnings conditioned upon past earning and past prices if earnings are the result of a compound process involving more than one stochastic variable. They characterize earnings as a mixture of two processes, where one process reflects the impact on earnings of events with no price implications and the other reflects the impact of events that imply price revisions.

Boatsman and Baskin (1981) analyze how precise P/E multiples are in valuation if one takes two different sets of companies in the same industry. They find that when they chose comparable companies with same kind of growth in earnings valuation are reduced as compared to companies chosen randomly.

Ou and Penman (1989) show that future earnings are a result of price information available in financial statements. The study evaluates suitable financial statement variables and the price ability in forecasting the earnings in future.

They also observe that changes in prices indicated by Collins, Kothari, and Rayburn (1987) and Beaver, Lambert and Ryan (1987) are not as good earnings forecaster as compared to predictors which rely on information contained in financial statement. Next, they show that the transitory earnings components as identified by information contained in financial statement also have impact on prices.

They observe that the predictable returns associated with P/E measures and those associated with accounting earnings predictors are negatively related. Thus, while P/E ratios and identified accounting numbers provide similar information about future earnings, they provide different information about future returns. The authors obtain their data from Compustat from a period of 1973 to 1983. The total number of firms obtained each year is approximately 2,500. The accounting indicator of future earnings through a scalar called as Pr using logit estimation technique is used for their testing.

They show that price to earnings comparisons are found to be relatively good predictors of earnings. They also observe that predictable returns associated with P/E measures and those associated with accounting earnings predictors are negatively related. Thus, while P/E ratios and identified accounting numbers provide similar information about future earnings, they provide different information about future returns. Finally the study proves that stock returns predicted by financial statement measure, Pr, are negatively correlated with stock returns predicted by P/E.

Alford (1992) evaluates how precise valuation is given by P/E multiples if comparable firms are chosen on the basis of earnings growth and size. He observes reduction in pricing errors when comparable companies are chosen narrowly.

Kaplan and Ruback (1995) evaluate discounted cash flow approach for highly levered transactions. They show that uncomplicated EBITDA multiples also result in the same valuation accuracy as one finds with DCF approach.

Penman (1996) interprets the P/E and market to book (P/B) ratio and describes how they articulate. The study also describes the role of book rate of return on equity (the ratio of their denominators) in the determination of ratios and the relation between them. For example, P/E has been interpreted as an earnings growth indicator, a risk measure and an earnings capitalization rate. Similarly, P/BV ratio explains mean stock returns, accompanied by conjectures that it is a proxy for risk or an indicator of distress, the difference between market and book leverage or mis-priced stocks.

Penmen (1997) extend his previous work to investigate approximate benchmark valuations that combine earnings and book value together. The study estimates weights such that a benchmark price=w1*book value+w2* earnings is estimated. Further it evaluates how robust these weights are over time.

The weights w1 and w2 are multiples applied to earnings and book value but in such a way as to accommodate the two numbers implied jointly. Book value is the balance sheet measure of net assets that generate earnings and earnings is the income statement measure of returns from these assets. So they probably have information in common but may also have information the other does not have. This study investigates how the different information provided by two multiples can be combined to get a single price. The study shows that estimated weights are robust over time and can be used to predict prices when applied out of sample. It also gives meaning to the weights and explains why they might vary over the differences between earnings and book value.

It takes a forecasting perspective similar to that in Ohlson (1995) and Feltham and Ohlson (1995). Price is viewed as based on expected future earnings so current earnings and book value inform about price because they forecast future earnings. Accordingly, the weights that combine earnings and book value into a composite valuation are also weights that combine forecasts of future earnings based on each separately into a composite forecast. The weights indicate how much emphasis one puts on current earnings as indicative of future earnings and how much one emphasizes the current book value.

However, the analysis differs from the Ohlson and Feltham and Ohlson Models in that weights are shown to be changing over time, as periodic earnings and book values change, rather than fixed firm parameters that are applied irrespective of level of earnings relative to book value. The paper also shows that the weights that combine earnings and book value into price give an indication of the P/E and P/BV ratios, the multiples applied to each separately. Indeed, the analyses yields revised benchmarks for these multipliers.

Baker and Ruback (1995) analyze industry multiples for the S&P 500 in 1995. The study focuses on two implementation challenges when using valuation multiples: how to estimate the industry multiple and how to choose a measure of financial performance as a basis of substitutability. They simultaneously evaluate sample minimum variance and error specification multiples across twenty two industries using Gibbs sampling. Further, they reflect on the performance of four common multiples: the harmonic mean, the median, the value-weighted mean, and the simple mean. They find that harmonic mean is a close approximation to the Gibbs minimum variance estimates.

Tasker [1998] analyzes acquisition transactions to find out all industry patterns used for selection by investment bankers and analysts. Beatty, Riffe, and Thompson [1999] evaluate pair-wise combination of multiples derived from total assets, dividends, earnings and book value. They find that combination of book and earnings multiples results in best performance wherein weight is derived using harmonic mean.

Baker and Ruback [1999] analyze comparative performance of multiples based on Sales, EBIT and EBITDA. They also evaluate the econometric problems arising in computing industry multiples. Like Beatty, Riffe and Thomson (1999) they also find harmonic mean to be close to minimum variance estimates. Further, they show that multiples based on EBITDA perform best in comparison to EBIT and Sales using harmonic mean estimator.

Kim and Ritter [1999] observe that in terms of valuation accuracy forward P/E multiples are best among all. They show that EPS forecast for next year dominates the current year EPS forecast.

Liu, Nissim, and Thomas (2001a) evaluate broad list of price multiples to determine the best value driver in explaining the price of a firm. They try to find out which multiple is close to observed stock price where in they forecast price by multiplying a value driver with the corresponding multiple. Apart from studying the multiples they also analyze the reasons of performance variation in different sectors over time and if performance can be improved by using different approaches in estimating multiples.

Liu, Nissim and Thomas (2002b) expand their erstwhile work for ten different sets of countries. They analyzed price multiples based on earnings, sales, cash-flows and dividends. The methodology adopted is same as in their previous work. However, period covered is from March 1976 to June 2001. They show earnings as a value driver performs best for the 10 countries whereas dividend and cash-flow comes in between followed by sales as the worst performer in forecasting prices. They also observe that post 1997 all the value drivers are declining in performance due to emerging heterogeneity of companies within the same industry group.

Liu, Nissim and Thomas (2005) compare cash-flow multiples and earnings multiples to find out the best among the two. The sample period is from January 1987 to September 2004 and methodology remains same as in their previous work. They find, that contrary to the popular view that cash-flows perform better than earnings; stock prices are better explained by earnings. The reason for better performance of earnings is the large transitory component of reported cash flows.

Huang, Tsai and Chen (2007) decompose the price to earning multiple into a residual component and a fundamental component to evaluate P/E anomaly. They investigate if the reversal in performance of the P/E ratios and stock return is due to fundamentals or due to investor psychology. They took data of NYSE firms from 1982 to 2002. They find that both macroeconomic factors and firm specific factors determine P/E multiples. Finally, they observe that extreme portfolios constructed based upon residual P/E ratios, exhibit performance reversals only for portfolios constructed using top residual P/E ratios and hence it supports the over-optimism hypothesis of the P/E anomaly. Conversely, the bottom residual P/E portfolios show no sign of performance reversals, indicating the lack of over pessimism. Thus, it can be explained by changing firm and economic fundamentals, not investor overreaction.

Da and Schaumburg (2008) use the data of target price announcement from 1997-2004 to show that investors get valuable information from within industry relative valuation included in analysts target price as compared to absolute information.

7.2 Literature on Emerging Markets including India

In emerging markets also some research has been done on relative valuation. Gupta, Jain and Gupta (1998) study market price to earning ratio and show its importance in getting market signals. They also give a new approach to evaluate different levels of P/E ratios in the analysis of various companies and market as a whole. The analysis covers the period from 1980 to 1996.The study comprised two sets of partially overlapping analyses, one focusing on long-term historical change in the P/E ratio from 1980 to 1994 and the other focusing on its short-term behaviour during recent years i.e. 1990 to 1996. The long-term historical analyses covers around 300-500 companies each year from the official directory of Bombay Stock Exchange.

Dhankar and Kumar (2007) measure the performance of a set of portfolios, which are based on P/E of stocks. The study involves the analysis of monthly data of price earnings of the composite portfolio of BSE 100 companies. The data is collected from PROWESS for the period of June 1996 to May 2006 and there are three non overlapping sub periods (June 1996-December 19999, January 2000 to December 2002, and January 2003 to May 2005). The BSE 100 companies are taken as sample. The study refutes the efficient market hypothesis because of the poor performance of high P/E ratios. It also questions the validity of capital asset pricing model on the basis of inconsistent relationship between portfolios return and market risk. It determines that portfolios with low market risk have outperformed the portfolios with high market risk.

The study analyzes the 100 companies of BSE 100 which represents 75 percent market capitalization that includes actively traded large, mid and small cap stocks. All the 100 stocks are arranged in ascending order on the basis of median P/E ratio. Subsequently, 10 portfolios each comprising 10 stocks are constructed. The portfolio, which occupies first rank, comprises 10 stocks with the least median P/E ratio. Portfolio placed second comprises 10 stocks with second least median P/E ratios and so on. Portfolio at the tenth place comprises 10 stocks with highest median P/E ratios. To depict the characteristic of P/E portfolios separate estimates are done for quartile 1, quartile 3 and the inter-quartile range. To show the variation in P/E ratio, Quartile deviation and coefficient of quartile are estimated. A low coefficient of quartile deviation exhibits uniformity or small variation in the distribution of P/E ratios.

According to the efficient market hypothesis, portfolio P10 should comparatively yield higher return than portfolio P9, P9 should yield higher return than portfolio P8, and so on. Similarly, Portfolio P1 should yield least return in comparison to other portfolios. Consequently, portfolio expected return should go up as one moves from low market risk portfolio P1 to high market risk portfolio P10, which should have maximum return. To construct market portfolios, the return of ten portfolios were integrated with the market return. The expected return of the stock is regressed to the return of market in time period t.

The study reveals that the expected return of portfolios P2, P4 and P5 show consistency with their corresponding P/E ratios. The expected return of portfolios went up from low P/E portfolios to high P/E portfolios, but no consistency is observed in the increase of return with corresponding P/E ratios. The relationship between portfolio market risk and return is supposed to be positive and linear. The correlation coefficient between the two is found to be 0.31 which is significant at 40 percent level of significance. The important evidence which flows from the result was that in all portfolios, beta and return were significant at 5 percent level.

To help provide an insight into the efficiency of these portfolios and validation of efficient market hypothesis and capital asset pricing model, a set of ten portfolios are tested in three non overlapping periods. The period June 1996 to May 2005, is divided into three sub period, covering June 1996-December 1999, January 2000-December 2002, and January 2003- May 2005. These three sub periods are selected because they exhibited successive three economic phases in Indian economy.

The period June 1996 to December 1999 exhibits decline phase in the economy with 6.3 percent average growth rate. Period January 2000 to December 2002 outlines the recession phase in the economy with 4.3 percent growth rate. Indian economy, on the other hand was on growth phase during January 2003 to May 2005 with 7.7 percent growth rate. No consistency is observed in expected returns of portfolios to their P/E ratios during decline phase. However, portfolio expected return is showing increasing tendency from low P/E to high P/E portfolios. All the portfolios expected return and beta are significant at least at 10 percent level.

During recession phase the portfolio expected return goes up as one moves from low P/E portfolio to high P/E portfolio, but no consistency in portfolios return were observed; as portfolio P3 and P4 had low P/E , yet yield comparatively high return over the high P/E portfolio P6 and P7. Further it is shown that the correlation coefficient between portfolios expected return and market risk was fairly high. It is significant at 5 percent level. Under growth phase it is observed that portfolio expected return exhibits declining tendency with movement form low P/E portfolio to high P/E portfolio.

The observation is consistent with Basu (1977) findings, where he observes that average annual rate of return declines as one moves from low P/E portfolios to high P/E portfolio. The correlation coefficient between portfolios expected returns and market risk, is high and significant at 5 percent level. It indicates that the risk aversion tendency of investors makes them demand high return for high market risk.

The results of the research work are relevant form the policy making point of view, as a large number of investors make their investment decisions and forecast the future performance of stocks by considering the P/E ratios. The findings of the study question the validation of investment decisions based on the P/E ratios. The cross sectional test of 10 P/E portfolios under decline and recession phases in Indian economy bring out that portfolio expected return has increase, as one moves from the low P/E portfolio to high P/E portfolio, however the rise in return is not continuous.

On the contrary, in the growth phase, portfolio expected return show declining tendency as one moves from low P/E portfolio to high P/E portfolio. An important finding in the study is that Indian stock market has failed to absorb new information, and has not reflected instantaneous response in the stock returns. The findings of the pooled period and three sub periods fail to establish any relationship between P/E ratios and their portfolio performance. This leads to question the validity of efficient market hypothesis. It holds the validation of capital asset pricing model in Indian stock market, as the descriptor of portfolio return corresponding to market risk.

Irina, Alexander and Ivan (2007) prove that using peers from developed markets would overstate the estimation of equity value in emerging market, because companies from emerging markets are subject to various factors such as political, economic risks, low level of corporate governance, high negative skewness, and thus require an adequate discount. This in turn, implies a necessity for an adjustment factor, which shows the difference in the level of multiples between developed and emerging market holding financials constant. In this study they introduce additional cross sectional method to calculate adjustment factor. They also calculate standard country dummy method. The study analyzes Russian and US data for the period of 2001- 2006 and find that the adjustment is very low for all multiples for all specifications, i.e. the difference in multiples, which is not explained by fundamentals, is very large. It starts from -80 percent-90 percent in 2001 and slowly declines to -30 percent-60 percent in 2005-06.

In sum, lot of work has been done in matured markets with regards to price multiples. The studies have been conducted to analyze historical price multiples and also attempt has been made to find out best historical price multiple vis-à-vis P/E, P/BV, P/CF and P/S ratios. The research work has been carried out for forward multiples as well. The researchers have also tried to combined price multiples to find out whether combination of price multiples provide better results in equity valuation when compared to standalone multiples.

A lot of work has also been conducted for industry or

sector multiples as well as to analyze fundamental determinants of price multiples. On the other hand in the emerging markets, including India, no comprehensive investigation of price multiples has been done. The emerging market literature is confined to P/E ratios. There has been no conclusive research done on other price multiples like P/BV ratios, P/CF ratios or P/Sales ratios to name a few.

8

Equity Valuation: Theoretical Framework

8.1 Concept of Valuation

Value is the defining dimension of measurement in a market economy. People make investments in various asset classes with the expectation that when they sell, the value of each investment will have grown by a sufficient amount above its cost to compensate them for the risk they undertook. It remains true for all types of investments, be they be real assets like properties or financial assets like bank accounts, bonds, shares or derivatives. Oscar Wild, the Spanish poet and writer, once depicted a cynic as a person who "knows the price of everything but value of nothing".

The term valuation may be used by various investors differently according to needs. For example investment philosophy of investor determines the importance of valuation. For passive management of a portfolio it has very narrow role, while for active management valuation plays a significant role. In equity valuation all investors are concerned with the question of value of common stock. The expected return from the stock depends on the under or over valuation of stock at the time of purchase. There are various techniques of valuing stock which predominantly comprise of discounted cash flow (DCF) models, relative valuation and technical analysis. Then there are information traders who believe in market inefficiencies and try to take advantage of insider trading or asymmetric flow of news and make trading gains.

8.2 Approaches to Valuation

There have been numerous approaches to valuation which are being used by market participants. However predominant among them are DCF Approach, Relative Valuation, Contingent claim valuation and technical analysis. DCF is based on fundamentals of the company which mainly comprise of cash flows, risk and growth. Relative valuation on the other hand is based on how similar assets are priced in market. It is also known as price multiples approach and mainly comprises of Price to Earnings (P/E) ratio, Price to Cash Flow (P/CF) ratio, Price to Book Value (P/BV) ratio and Price to Sales (P/S) ratio. Contingent claim valuation is used in case of assets which share option characteristics by using option pricing models. Technical analysts, on the other hand are least bothered about the fundamentals. They believe that it is the force of demand and supply that derives price and by looking at past prices and volumes one can forecast future price.

8.2.1 Discounted Cash Flow Valuation (DCF): DCF approach is the key building block for almost all the other techniques in valuation. It is based on the important premise that cash flows received by a firm at different time intervals have different value. It is also known as fundamental approach to valuation and its roots go back to the times of ancient Greeks, who calculated and used the concept of simple and compound interest. In DCF the value of an asset is determined by the magnitude and the timing of the cash flows it is expected to generate.

DCF has its foundation in the present value rule, where the value of any asset is the present value of expected future cash-flows that the asset generates.

$$\text{Value} = \sum_{t=1}^{t=n} \frac{CFt}{(1+r)^t}$$

where, n = Life of the asset

CFt = Cash Flow in period t

r = Discount rate reflecting the riskiness of the estimated cash-flows

Specifically, the use of DCF valuation entails a three step process:

1. *Forecast the amount and timing of cash flows*: It involves forecasting the amount and timing of anticipated future cash flows. The basic question to be asked here is How much cash flow the project is expected to generate and when?
2. *Estimate a risk appropriate discount rate i.e. combine debt and equity discount rates to get WACC (weighted average cost of capital)*: Here, the role of analyst is to find out the appropriate discount rate to be used in discounting future cash flows to their present value.
3. *Discount the cash flows*: In the last step the future cash flows are discounted back to get their intrinsic value by using the discount rate calculated in step 2.

Thus, DCF approach calculates the intrinsic value of an asset and when compared with the market price it helps in finding out whether the asset is overpriced or under-priced. DCF can be used primarily for three kinds of valuations: (a) to value the entire firm, (b) to value stakes of equity shareholders in the company, and (c) to value firm in pieces.

DCF approach broadly has three variants viz. dividend discount models, free cash flow to equity model and free cash flow to firm model. Analyst can rely on this approach for assets who are having positive cash flows and which can be estimated with reasonable degree of accuracy. Under certain situations it becomes difficult to value assets using DCF approach like for troubled firms having negative earnings will be difficult to be valued using DCF. Similarly, firms with unutilized assets, firms with patent or product options and firms in the process of restructuring will be having difficulty in using DCF as a valuation technique.

8.2.2 Contingent Claim Valuation: Option pricing models or real options as they are called, exist for any investment in which managers have the ability to exercise discretion. This discretion may involve timing issues such as determining when to initiate a new project or shut down an old project. They can also be exercised over how an existing investment is operated like mangers can respond to changing product demand by altering the product mix and can respond to changing price by changing the mix of inputs they use.

Effectively, when one values real options we are in a sense determining the value that an active management team can add when it responds in a dynamic way to a changing environment. Real options contribute to an investment's value whenever the following two conditions hold: (i) the environment is uncertain, and (ii) managers can respond to changing circumstances by altering the way the investment is implemented and or managed. The application of real options varies across industries and even firms within industries. Like real option analysis is used extensively in energy and natural resources industries using complicated techniques. In other industries real options are evaluated with approaches that are less sophisticated are real estate development. Predominantly, there are three approaches being used to value assets using real options:

1. The first approach is binomial lattice approach to value financial options.
2. The second approach is the application of real option formula like Black-Scholes formula. However, these approaches are not used by industry but they can a useful starting point to determine whether a more refined analysis is warranted.
3. The last approach is simulation analysis that is capable of dealing with most complicated investments.

The real options are difficult to be used in cases where the financial or the real asset has no traded value which will lead to greater estimation errors if one uses real options.

8.2.3 Technical Analysis: The philosophy behind technical analysis is in sharp contrast to fundamental valuation which involves making decisions based on examination of fundamental factors like cash flows, risk and growth. Technical analysis involves the examination of past market data like prices and volumes of trading, which helps in discovering future prices. Technical analyst see no need to study the multitude of economic, industry and company variables to arrive at an estimate of future price because they believe that past price movements will signal future price movements. Technical analysis can be broken down into three essential parts:

1. **Sentiments:** They monitor the actions of different market participants like brokers, mutual funds, institutional investors etc. The basis of examining these groups is that different groups of investors are consistent in their actions at major market turning points.
2. **Flow of Funds:** It analyses the financial position of various investor groups in an attempt to measure their potential capacity for buying or selling shares. It is concerned with trends in mutual fund cash positions, insurance companies, bank trusts etc.
3. **Market Structure:** Market structure indicators monitor the various price indexes, market breadth, cycles and volumes in order to evaluate the position of markets.

To sum up, technical analysis is based on published capital market data as opposed to fundamental data. Users of technical analysis work on the premise that market prices adjust to the equilibrium price and believe that the process by which prices adjust to new information is one of gradual adjustment towards a new equilibrium price.

8.3 Relative Valuation

All investors are concerned with the question of the value of common stock. The return which any investor gets from buying security depends upon whether the security at the time of purchase was overvalued or under valued. Although analysts talk mostly about discounted cash-flow valuation but the reality is that most valuations being done practically are relative valuations. The value of most assets, from the property one put his money in to or the financial assets in which one invests, depend upon how other comparable assets fetch price in their respective markets.

Price multiples are ratios of a stock's market price to some measure of value per share. Price multiples have the appealing qualities of simplicity in use and ease in communication. From newspapers columns to research reports, the investor constantly sees them in action. It is based on the assumption that the firm being valued should be priced depending upon how other firms in the same industry are priced. It is based upon the hypothesis that the firms in the same industry are comparable and that on average the market prices these firms correctly. The prominent price multiples used in relative valuation are P/E ratios, P/CF ratios, P/BV ratios and P/S ratios. A firm is said to be undervalued if it's respective price multiple is lower than that of the industry multiple in which the firm operates. If the value of the price multiple is more than that of industry average the firm is said to be over valued.

Relative valuation works on two principles. The first and foremost principle is that we have to standardize the prices in order to find out the value which an asset carries. This can be done by developing relationship of prices with regards to value drivers like earnings, cash flows, book value or sales and forming price multiples. The other and somewhat difficult task is to find out comparable companies which can have same business risk, similar cash flows and growth potentials as that of the firm being valued.

8.3.1 Reasons for Popularity: Relative valuation is used as a major technique in valuations because it requires lesser amount of assumptions and is easy to calculate. Another reason for its popularity is that it is easily presented and understood by clients in comparison to other tools. Most of the pitch books prepared by investment bankers or reports prepared by brokers are presented to their clients using relative valuation. Lastly, it reflects the present temper of the market as it tries to value asset on a relative basis.

8.3.2 Drawbacks of Relative Valuation: One of the major difficulties in relative valuation is to find out comparable firm. If the comparable firms chosen are different with respect to their fundamentals, then valuation given by such firms may give misleading results. Another pitfall of relative valuation is that it reveals how the markets at present are pricing the asset. It will give the true value if markets are efficient. But in inefficient markets it will either over value or under value the shares.

8.3.3 Basic Steps in Relative Valuation: In order to prudently apply multiples it is imperative to follow four basic steps. In the first instance one should be certain that price multiples are defined consistently. Next, one should be clear with the descriptive analysis of the price multiples. After this, one should evaluate if the multiples are determined by their respective fundaments and how do they react with the change in fundamentals. Lastly, the comparable firms chosen should be the right ones to get accuracy in valuation. The four steps talk about abovc arc discusscd bclow in bricf:

A. Definitional Tests: By applying this test one is trying to understand how price multiples have been defined. It is of paramount importance that multiples across firms in a valuation should be defined consistently. Likewise, when analysts use P/E, there may be different variants used by different analysts. One analyst may take closing prices in numerator whereas the other may take average price of the last six months or a year. Similarly, EPS may be taken as a trailing four quarters EPS or last year's EPS or forecasted EPS.

Similarly, multiples may be based on equity value or firm value. When we are trying to calculate equity value multiples used are based on market price whereas if we are trying to value firm then firm multiples like enterprise value (EV) should be taken in numerator. Similarly, denominator should also match up to numerator i.e. if we are calculating equity value then denominator should be EPS but if we are trying to calculate firm value it should be EBITDA or some other firm measure.

B. Descriptional Tests: The second important test while

using multiples is to understand the descriptive. Like before, using multiples one should be very clear about the distributional properties as well as about high and low values of that multiple in industry or in market. It is imperative to evaluate the impact which outliers will have on average values and treat them accordingly. Most of the market analysts are specialists for their respective sectors and know about various companies in their respective sectors.

However, they also need to know how multiples are distributed across market. They should understand about the distributional properties of multiples across market. We generally, use averages and standard deviation of multiples as parameters to be used in equity valuation. But we can use mean values only if price multiples tend to form normal distributions. If price multiple distributions are skewed and non normal, it is better to use median values as compared to averages. So, it is of paramount importance to test the distributional properties of multiples before using them.

There are various pitfalls due to which it becomes difficult to use multiples in valuation. Like, if a company is having negative EPS then it is not possible to apply P/E ratio. Therefore, if someone is analyzing price multiples for a sector he should remove negative P/E ratio companies from the sample. But since, companies with negative EPS are removed, the average price multiple for the sector will be biased upward. One can deal with such bias in one of the following ways. First is to adjust the average P/E to a lower value to reflect the adjustment made for removing companies from the list. Other way is to sum up the market value of all the companies in the sample and divide them by the aggregate net income value.

C. Analytical Tests: Here, one tries to find out the fundamental determinants of the price multiples and how the changes in fundamentals affect price multiples.

All the price multiples whether they are for earnings, cash flows, book value or sales are governed by the same fundamental determinants i.e. cash flows, risk and growth.

Cash flows and growth have the positive impact on multiples whereas risk has negative impact on the price multiples.

We can find out the fundamental determinants of price multiples using the stable growth dividend discount model as given by Gordon:

Value of equity = Po = $DPS_1/k_e - g$

where, DPS_1 is the expected dividend next year, k_e is the cost of equity and g is the expected stable growth rate.

After understanding the fundamental determinants of respective price multiples it becomes important to understand their relationship with price multiples. For example, if one says that price multiple for firms in their growth stage should be high, then one should also understand how high it is with regards to sector. To analyze it, one should know the effect on P/E with respect to the change in growth rate. Similarly, one should know how the changes in other determinants affect the price multiple.

D. Application Tests: Another important step in relative valuation is to find out comparable firms to be used in valuation. Generally, analysts tend to take comparable firms as the firms in the same industry. Ideally, a comparable firm should be one which is having the same kind of risk, cash flow potential and growth prospects. However, it is very difficult to find such a firm even within the same industry. On the other hand, it may be possible that some firm in other industry may have same kind of fundamentals. Therefore, a pharmaceutical firm can be valued using an IT firm as comparable provided the IT firm has same fundamental factors.

If one can find comparable firms in abundance in the same industry then, he can put filters like firms with similar size to be chosen as comparable firm. However, if there are not sufficient number of firms available in the same industry one can look out for firms outside the industry with the similar fundamentals. In developed countries like United States, one rarely encounters such a problem because there are fairly large number of listed companies in every sector. But in emerging markets like India, one has to grapple with such a problem because there are few sectors like media and publishing where still there are very few listed firms.

8.4 Prominent Price Multiples

8.4.1 Price Earnings Ratio: Predominantly, P/E ratio is the most widely used ratio in comparison to all other price multiples. It is simple to calculate i.e. by dividing Price by the EPS, i.e.

P/E = Earnings per share/Market Price per share.

As in other price multiples, market price is readily determinable and easy to observe. But the denominator, EPS, is based on complex rules of accrual accounting and presents important interpretation issues. For example, firms which are in their high growth phase, the PE ratio can be very different depending upon which measure of earnings per share is used.

The biggest rationale for using P/E ratio is that earning power is the chief driver of investment value and P/E is widely recognized as used by investors. However, it becomes difficult to apply P/E if EPS is a negative number. Another difficulty with P/E is that management may distort it through various accounting policies.

8.4.2 Book Value Multiples: The ratio of market price to book value per share (P/BV), has along history of use in valuation practice. According to the Merrill Lynch Institutional Factor Survey for the years 1989 to 2001, P/BV has been the second most popular price multiple (after P/E) to be used among institutional investors. In the P/E ratio the value driver, namely EPS, used in denominator is a flow variable taken from the income statement. In contrast, the measure of value in P/B's denominator (book value) is a stock variable coming from the balance sheet. Intuitively, book value per share attempts to represent the investment that common shareholders have made in the company, on a per share basis. To define book value per share we first find shareholders' equity (Total Assets-Total Liabilities) and subtract any amount attributed towards preference share holders. Dividing book value by the number of common stock shares outstanding, we obtain book value per share, the denominator in the P/BV ratio. The price to book ratio is computed by dividing the market price per share by the current book value of equity per share.

Price to Book Ratio = P/BV [Price per share/Book value of equity per share].

One of the most important rationales for using P/BV ratio is that book value is a cumulative balance sheet amount and is generally a positive number. The other factor which goes in favour of book value is that book value is a more stable number as compared to price which is more volatile. Book value per share has been viewed as an appropriate measure for valuing companies composed of chiefly liquid assets like finance, investment, insurance and banking institutions.

However, there are certain disadvantages associated with book value. Like other assets, such as human resources, besides those recognized in accounting, may be of critical importance. P/BV can be misleading as a valuation indicator when significant differences exist among companies examined in terms of level of assets used. Accounting effects like expensing research and development (R&D) investment, by some companies can impair comparability of book value across companies and countries. Another demerit is that book value being the historical measure does not reflect the current value of assets.

8.4.3 Price to Sales Ratio: It evaluates the value of a firm by taking sales as a value driver. One of the important rationales for taking this ratio is that sales being the top line number are less subject to distortions or manipulations than are other fundamentals such as EPS or book value. EPS numbers can be distorted by management by using discretionary accounting decisions concerning expenses like depreciation. Another reason for using P/S ratio is that EPS can at times like for new firms or distressed firms become negative, however sales can become negative.

Hence, for such companies it is the viable alternative to P/E. P/S is also generally more stable than P/E because sales are more stable which reflects operating and financial leverage. Thus, P/S will be more meaningful when EPS numbers are abnormally high or low. However, it also suffers from some limitations. Like a business may show high growth in sales even when it is not operating profitably as judged by earnings and cash flow from operations. Secondly, although relatively robust with manipulations, revenue practices offer the potential to distort P/S.

9

Integration of Financial Markets

9.1 Heterogeneous Nature of Financial Markets

Various financial market segments are not uniform as they trade in a variety of instruments which differ in terms of risk and liquidity. Financial markets are heterogeneous due to following reasons:

- Some market segments are national, whereas others are international in nature, depending on where financial transactions occur among participants within a country's geographic boundary or across the border. Generally, money and credit market segments involving participation of banks and other financial institutions operating within a country's boundary are national in character. Conversely, foreign exchange markets dealing with cross-border transactions and stock markets with cross-listings of securities and participation of foreign institutional investors are international in nature.
- Financial markets differ in terms of depth and liquidity. For instance, money market instruments are more liquid, while bonds in the capital markets are less liquid.
- Financial markets differ in terms of economic nature of instruments catering to various needs of economic agents. For instance, a distinction can be made between saving, investment, credit and derivative instruments.
- Financial markets are differentiated in terms of risk profile of instruments such as government bonds, which do not involve default and credit risks, and corporate bonds, which are relatively more risky in nature. Integration of market segments, thus, reflects an investor's attitude towards risk and the trade-off between risk and return on assets.

- Market participants in different financial markets could be different such as banks, non-bank financial institutions, including mutual funds, insurance companies, mortgage institutions and specialised long-term financial institutions.

9.2 Meaning of Financial Integration

Integration of financial markets is a process of unifying markets and enabling convergence of risk-adjusted returns on the assets of similar maturity across the markets. The process of integration is facilitated by an unimpeded access of participants to various market segments. Financial markets all over the world have witnessed growing integration within as well as across boundaries, spurred by deregulation, globalisation and advances in information technology. Central banks in various parts of the world have made concerted efforts to develop financial markets, especially after the experience of several financial crises in the 1990s.

Expectedly, financial markets tend to be better integrated in developed countries. At the same time, deregulation in developing countries has led to removal of restrictions on pricing of various financial assets, which is one of the pre-requisites for market integration.

Financial market integration encompasses a complex interplay of various factors such as policy initiatives, structure and growth of financial intermediaries, organic linkages among market participants and the preference of savers and investors for financial instruments. The study of integration of financial markets must keep in view the heterogeneity of markets, dimensions of integration, measurement issues and perceived benefits and risks of integration.

Financial market integration at the theoretical level has been postulated in several ways. The most popular economic principles of financial integration include the law of one price, term structure of interest rates, parity conditions such as purchasing power parity, covered and uncovered interest parity conditions, capital asset price model and arbitrage price theory.

9.3 Dimensions of Financial Market Integration

Broadly, financial market integration occurs in three dimensions, nationally, regionally and globally. From an alternative perspective, financial market integration could take place horizontally and vertically. In the horizontal integration, inter-linkages occur among domestic financial market segments, while vertical integration occurs between domestic markets and regional/international financial markets.

9.3.1 Domestic Financial Integration: It entails horizontal linkages of various segments, reflecting portfolio diversification by savers, investors and intermediaries. Under horizontal integration, market interest rates typically revolve around a basic reference rate, which is defined as the price of a short-term low-risk financial instrument in a competitive and liquid market. Domestic markets may be closely integrated because intermediaries operate simultaneously in various market segments; for instance, commercial banks operate in both the saving (deposit) and loan markets.

9.3.2 Regional Financial Integration: It occurs due to ties between a given region and the major financial centre serving that region. Economic integration might be easier to achieve at a regional level due to network externalities and the tendency of market makers to concentrate in certain geographical centres. Furthermore, regional financial integration can be an important means of developing local financial markets, for instance, through peer pressure to strengthen institutions and upgrade local practices.

9.3.3 Global Financial Integration: It refers to the opening up of domestic markets and institutions to the free cross-border flow of capital and financial services by removing barriers such as capital controls and withholding taxes. A deeper dimension of global integration entails removing obstacles to movement of people, technology and market participants across border. Global integration is promoted through harmonisation of national standards and laws, either through the adoption of commonly agreed minimum standards or the mutual recognition of standards.

9.4 Measures of Financial Integration

Indicators of financial integration can be classified into *de jure* and *de facto* measures.

The existence of legal restrictions on trade and capital flows across border as well as market segments is the most frequently used *de jure* indicators. However, these indicators have several shortcomings as restrictions may not be binding, or they are not respected. They may not cover a specific aspect of all possible impediments to financial integration.

De facto indicators of financial integration are usually based either on prices or quantities. The commonly used price-based measures for gauging price equalisation and convergence of market segments include cross-market spreads, correlation among various interest rates, tests of common trend in the term structure of interest rates and volatility transmission. Interest rate spreads between the official short-term rate and a benchmark short-term market instrument on the one hand, and various other market interest rates on the other, are used for measuring price convergence and effectiveness of policy. Price-related measures also include covered and uncovered interest rate parity as well as asset price correlations between countries.

There are, however, serious practical problems in using prices to measure regional or global financial integration, particularly in developing countries. This is because prices may move together because of a common external factor or because of similar macroeconomic fundamentals and not because of market integration. Moreover, prices may be affected by differences in currency, credit and liquidity risks, implying different price movements even if there is a substantial degree of financial integration.

9.5 Benefits and Risks of Financial Integration

Though financial integration provides several benefits, it

also involves various risks. The benefits and costs of financial market integration depend on the degree of domestic financial market integration, international financial integration and financial development. Evaluating the benefits and risks of financial market integration is a complex issue, particularly in an economy with open capital account.

9.5.1 Benefits: The benefits of global integration depend on size, composition, and quality of capital flows. Global financial integration involves direct and indirect or collateral benefits. Analytical arguments supporting financial openness revolve around main considerations such as the benefits of international risk sharing for consumption smoothing, the positive impact of capital flows on domestic investment and growth, enhanced macroeconomic discipline and increased efficiency as well as greater stability of the domestic financial system associated with financial openness. International financial integration could positively affect total factor productivity. Financial openness may increase the depth and breadth of domestic financial markets and lead to an increase in the degree of efficiency of the financial intermediation process by lowering costs and excessive profits associated with monopolistic and cartelised markets, thereby lowering the cost of investment and improving the resource allocation.

9.5.2 Risks: Financial market integration also poses some risks and entails costs. A major risk is that of contagion, which was evident in the case of East Asian crisis and the recent global financial turmoil. Increased domestic and international integration accentuates the risk of contagion as problems in one market segment are likely to be transmitted to other markets with the potential to cause systemic instability.

In the context of globalisation, potential costs include: (a) high degree of concentration of capital flows, (b) misallocation of flows which may hamper their growth effects and exacerbate domestic distortions; (c) loss of macroeconomic stability, (d) pro-cyclical nature of short-term capital flows and the risk of abrupt reversals, (e) a high degree of volatility of capital flows which relates in part to herding and contagion effects, and (f) risks associated with foreign bank penetration.

Direct investment tends to be less volatile than other forms of capital flows. Volatility of capital flows translates into exchange rate instability (under flexible exchange rate) or large fluctuations in official reserves (under a pegged exchange rate regime). Nominal exchange rate volatility may hamper expansion of exports if appropriate hedging techniques are not available to exporters. Large capital inflows can also lead to rapid monetary expansion, inflationary pressures, real exchange rate appreciation and widening of current account deficits.

The nature of optimal integration is highly country-specific and contextual. Financial integration needs to be approached cautiously, preferably within the framework of a plausible roadmap that is drawn up embodying the country-specific context and institutional features.

On balance, there appears to be a greater advantage in well-managed and appropriate integration into the global process, which implies not large-scale but more effective interventions by the authorities.

9.6 Need for Integration of Domestic Financial Markets

Integration of financial markets assumes importance due to the following reasons:

1. Efficient and integrated financial markets constitute an important vehicle for promoting domestic savings, investment and consequently economic growth.
2. Financial market integration, by enhancing competition and efficiency of intermediaries in their operations and allocation of resources, contributes to financial stability.
3. Integrated markets serve as a conduit for authorities to transmit important price signals.
4. Integrated financial markets induce market discipline and informational efficiency.
5. Market integration promotes the adoption of modern

technology and payment systems to achieve cost effective financial intermediation services.

6. Integrated markets lead to innovations and cost effective intermediation, thereby improving access to financial services for members of the public, institutions and companies alike.
7. Financial market integration fosters the necessary condition for financial sector of a country to emerge as an international or a regional financial centre.

An important objective of reforms in India has been to integrate the various segments of the financial market for bringing about a transformation in the structure of markets, reducing arbitrage opportunities, achieving higher level of efficiency in market operation of intermediaries and increasing efficacy of monetary policy in the economy. Efficient allocation of funds across the financial sector and uniformity in the pricing of various financial products through greater inter-linkages of financial markets has been the basic emphasis of monetary policy.

In the domestic sphere, integration of markets has been pursued through the following measures:

1. Strengthening competition.
2. Financial deepening with innovative instruments.
3. Easing of restrictions on flows or transactions.
4. Lowering of transaction costs.
5. Enhancing liquidity.

Financial markets in India have also increasingly integrated with the global financial system as a result of calibrated and gradual capital account liberalisation in keeping with the underlying macroeconomic developments, the state of readiness of the domestic financial system and the dynamics of international financial markets.

Until the early 1990s, India's financial sector was tightly controlled. Interest rates in all market segments were administered. The flow of funds between various market segments was restricted by extensive micro-regulations. There were also restrictions on participants operating in different market segments. Banks remained captive subscribers to government securities under statutory arrangements. The secondary market of government securities was dormant. In the equity market, new equity issues were governed by several complex regulations and restrictions. The secondary market trading of such equities lacked transparency and depth. The foreign exchange market remained extremely shallow as most transactions were governed by inflexible and low limits under exchange regulation and prior approval requirements. The exchange rate was linked to a basket of currencies. Although the financial sector grew considerably in the regulated environment, it could not achieve the desired level of efficiency. Compartmentalisation of activities of different types of financial intermediaries eliminated the scope for competition among existing financial intermediaries.

Financial markets reform initiated in the early 1990s focused on removal of structural bottlenecks, introduction of new players/instruments, free pricing of financial assets, relaxation of quantitative restrictions, improvement in trading, clearing and settlement practices and greater transparency. Other policy initiatives in the money, the foreign exchange, the government securities and the equity markets were aimed at strengthening institutions, greater transparency, encouraging good market practices, effective payment and settlement mechanism, rationalised tax structures and enabling legislative framework. Dismantling of various price and non-price controls in the financial system has facilitated the integration of financial markets.

Broadly, India's domestic financial market comprises the money market, the credit market, the government securities market, the equity market, the corporate debt market and the foreign exchange market. The channels of integration among various market segments differ. For instance, the Indian money and the foreign exchange markets are intrinsically linked in view of the presence of commercial banks and the short-term nature of both markets. The linkage is established through various channels such as banks borrowing in overseas markets, providing hedging facilities to corporates, accepting foreign currency deposits and acting as conduit for making payments for overseas merchant transactions.

The linkage between the call money and the government securities markets exists, as at times, large positions in government securities are funded through short-term borrowings. The foreign exchange market and the equity markets are linked through the operations of foreign institutional investors. The emerging linkages among the money, the government securities and the foreign exchange markets have at times necessitated the use of short-term monetary measures by the RBI for meeting demand-supply mismatches to curb volatility.

9.7 Measures Taken for Integration of Financial Markets

Broadly, integration of financial markets in India has been facilitated by various measures in the form of free pricing, widening of participation base in markets, introduction of new instruments and improvements in payment and settlement infrastructure.

9.7.1 Free Pricing: Free pricing in financial markets has been facilitated by various measures. These have included, *inter alia,* the following:

1. Freedom to banks to decide interest rate on deposits and credit.
2. Replacement of administered interest rates on government securities by an auction system.
3. Abolition of the system of *ad hoc* Treasury Bills in April 1997 and its replacement by the system of Ways and Means Advances (WMAs) with effect from April 1, 1997.
4. Shift in the exchange rate regime from a single-currency fixed-exchange rate system to a market-determined floating exchange rate regime.
5. Gradual liberalisation of the capital account.

6. Freedom to banks to determine interest rates (subject to a ceiling) and maturity period of Foreign Currency Non-Resident (FCNR) deposits (not exceeding three years).
7. Use derivative products for hedging risk.
8. In 1992, the Capital Issues (Control) Act, 1947 was repealed and with this ended all controls related to raising of resources from the market. Since then the issuers of securities can raise capital from the market without requiring any consent from any authority, either for making the issue or for pricing it.

9.7.2 Widening Participation: This has been achieved with the adoption of following measures:

1. Enhanced presence of foreign banks in line with India's commitment to the World Trade Organisation (WTO) under GATS, strengthened domestic and international markets inter-linkages, apart from increasing competition.
2. Participation in the call market was gradually widened by including non-banks such as financial institutions, non-banking financial companies, primary/satellite dealers, mutual funds and corporates (through primary dealers). The process of transformation of the call money market into a pure inter-bank market which commenced from May 2001, was completed in August 2005.
3. Foreign institutional investors (FIIs) have been allowed to participate in the Indian equity market and set up 100 percent debt funds to invest in government (Central and State) dated securities in both the primary and secondary markets. This provided a major thrust to the integration of domestic markets with international markets.
4. Linkage between the domestic foreign exchange market and the overseas market (vertical integration) has been facilitated by allowing banks/authorised dealers (ADs) to borrow and invest funds abroad (subject to certain limits), and to lend in foreign currency to companies in India for any productive purpose, giving them the choice to economise on interest cost and exchange risk. Exporters

also have the ability to substitute rupee credit for foreign currency credit.

5. Indian companies have been permitted to raise resources from abroad through American/Global Depository Receipts (ADRs/ GDRs), foreign currency convertible bonds (FCCBs) and external commercial borrowings (ECBs), thus, facilitating integration of domestic capital market with international capital market. The RBI allowed two-way fungibility of ADRs/GDRs in February 2002.
6. Corporates have been allowed to undertake active hedging operations by resorting to cancellation and rebooking of forward contracts, booking forward contracts based on past performance, using foreign currency options and forwards, and accessing foreign currency-rupee swap to manage longer-term exposures arising out of external commercial borrowings.
7. Integration of the credit market and the equity market has been strengthened by application of capital adequacy norms and allowing public sector banks to raise capital from the equity market up to 49 percent of their paid-up capital.

9.7.3 New Instruments: These have included the following:

1. Repurchase agreement (repo) has introduced as a tool of short-term liquidity adjustment. The liquidity adjustment facility (LAF) is open to banks and primary dealers. The LAF has emerged as a tool for both liquidity management and also signalling device for interest rates in the overnight market. Several new financial instruments such as inter-bank participation certificates (1988), certificates of deposit (June 1989), commercial paper (January 1990) and repos (December 1992) have been introduced. Collateralised borrowing and lending obligation (CBLO) and market repos have also emerged as money market instruments.
2. New auction-based instruments were introduced for 364-day, 182-day, 91-day and 14-day Treasury Bills, the zero

coupon bond and government of India dated securities. In the long-term segment, floating rate bonds (FRBs) benchmarked to the 364-day treasury bills yields and a 10-year loan with embedded call and put options exercisable on or after 5 years from the date of issue have been introduced.

3. Derivative products—such as forward rate agreements and interest rate swaps— were introduced in July 1999 to enable banks, FIs and PDs to hedge interest rate risks. A rupee-foreign currency swap market has been developed. ADs in the foreign exchange market have been permitted to use cross-currency options, interest rate and currency swaps, caps/collars and forward rate agreements (FRAs) in the international foreign exchange market, thereby facilitating the deepening of the market and enabling participants to diversify their risk.

9.7.4 Institutional Measures: These have included the following:

1. Institutions such as Discount and Finance House of India (DFHI), Securities Trading Corporation of India (STCI) and PDs have been allowed to participate in more than one market, thus strengthening the market inter-linkages.
2. The Clearing Corporation of India Ltd. (CCIL) was set up to act as a central counter-party to all trades involving foreign exchange, government securities and other debt instruments routed through it and to guarantee their settlement.

9.7.5 Technology, Payment and Settlement Infrastructure: Measures taken in this regard have included the following:

1. The Delivery-versus-Payment (DvP) system, the Negotiated Dealing System (NDS) and subsequently, the advanced Negotiated Dealing System–Order Matching (NDS-OM) trading module and the real time gross settlement system (RTGS) have brought about immense benefits in facilitating transactions and improving the

settlement process, which have helped in the integration of markets.

2. In the equity market, the floor-based open outcry trading system has been replaced by electronic trading system in all the stock exchanges.

Various segments of financial markets have become better integrated in the reform period, especially from the mid-1990s. As reforms in the financial markets progressed, linkages amongst various segments of market and between domestic and international markets improved.

9.8 Segment-wise Integration

9.8.1 Integration of the Government Securities Market: The existence of a *well*-developed government securities market is a pre-requisite for a market-based monetary policy and for facilitating financial market integration. The government securities market is also required to develop a domestic rupee yield curve, which could provide a credible benchmark for pricing of securities in other markets. The government securities market is increasingly getting integrated with other market segments as is reflected in the close co-movement of interest rates.

9.8.2 Integration of the Credit Market: The integration of the credit market with other money market segments has become more pronounced in recent years. Sustained credit demand has led to higher demand for funds, exerting some pressure on liquidity. This has been reflected in the decline in investment of banks in government securities and higher activity in all the money market segments such as inter-bank call money, collateralised borrowing and lending obligation (CBLO) and market repo rates.

9.8.3 Integration of the Foreign Exchange Market: The degree of integration of the foreign exchange market with other markets is largely determined by the degree of openness. At the cornerstone of the international finance, integration through foreign exchange market is characterised with the

Purchasing Power Parity (PPP) doctrine. According to the PPP, in the absence of restrictions on cross border movements of goods and services and assuming no transactions costs, commodity prices expressed in any single currency should be the same all over the world. In other words, the path of the nominal exchange rate should be guided by the developments in the domestic prices of goods and services *vis-à-vis* prices of the major trading partners.

9.8.4 Stock Market Integration: The equity market has relatively low and negative correlation with other market segments. The low correlation of the equity market with risk free instruments is indicative of greater volatility of stock returns and the existence of large equity risk premium. The large risk premium occurs when equity price movements cannot be rationalised with standard inter-temporal optimisation models of macroeconomic fundamentals such as consumption and savings. This can be on account of different participants in the equity and other financial markets. For instance, the common participation by banks in the money, the government, the foreign exchange and the credit markets ensures fairly high correlation among these segments. The exposure of banks to the capital market remains limited on account of restrictions due to prudential regulation.

To conclude, integration among various market segments has grown, especially in the recent period. Growing integration among various financial market segments has been accompanied by lower volatility of interest rates. Financial market integration reflects a dynamic interaction among various parameters such as liquidity, safety and risk, foreign exchange market development, private sector activity, and macroeconomic fundamentals. Alternatively, financial integration exhibits interaction among financial intermediaries, the Government, the private sector and the external sector.

Integrated financial markets are a key element in the transmission process and hence for the smooth conduct of monetary policy. Financial integration also leads to a better diversification of risks and makes a positive contribution to financial stability by improving the capacity of economies to absorb shocks.

On the other hand, fully integrated financial markets also pave the way for shocks to propagate more quickly among market participants, which could necessitate appropriate safeguards. To mitigate the risks and maximise benefits from financial integration, it is imperative that the financial markets are developed further. Enhanced co-operation among various regulatory authorities is also important for ensuring effective corrective action in an increasingly integrated environment. Further, it is necessary to establish further linkages amongst the various components of financial infrastructure—the trading, payment, clearing, settlement and custodian systems.

10

Capital Market and Global Financial Crisis

The global capital markets grew strongly in 2007 making an all time peak for equity and debt markets all over the world. Global financial depth, or the ratio of financial assets to GDP, rose to 359 percent in 2007 from 345 percent the year before. With the exception of government debt, all asset classes grew deeper. Accompanying financial asset growth in 2007 was acceleration in total cross-border capital flows, which rose to US$ 11.2 trillion. However, the financial crisis emanating from US caused downturns in all the major parts of world and put an end to the non-stop thirty years of expansion of global markets.

An interesting feature of the post-crisis scenario is that there is tremendous increase in cross-border investments outside the traditional centres of western world.

The capital markets in emerging economies until the mid-1980s generally suffered from the classic defects of bank denominated economies, i.e. shortage of equity capital, lack of liquidity, absence of foreign institutional investors, and lack of investor's confidence in the stock market. Since mid-1980s, the capital markets of developing economies started developing with financial liberalization and the easing of legislative and administrative barriers and the adoption of tougher regulations to boost investors' confidence.

With the beginning of financial liberalization in the developing countries, the flow of private foreign capital from the developed to developing countries has increased significantly and such flows of foreign capital have been mainly in the form of foreign direct investment and portfolio investment.

10.1 Causes of Global Financial Crisis

The global economic conditions deteriorated sharply during the year 2008 with several advanced economies experiencing their sharpest declines in the post-Second World War period. The associated adverse shocks spreading across developing countries accentuated the synchronised global slowdown. The global financial environment entered a crisis phase following the growing distress among large international financial institutions and the declaration of bankruptcy of Lehman Brothers.

The proximate cause of the current financial turbulence is attributed to the sub-prime mortgage sector in the US. At a fundamental level, however, the crisis could be ascribed to the persistence of large global imbalances which, in turn, were the outcome of long periods of excessively loose monetary policy in the major advanced economies during the early part of this decade.

10.1.1 Global Macro Imbalances: Global imbalances have been manifested through a substantial increase in the current account deficit of the US mirrored by the substantial surplus in Asia, particularly in China, and in oil exporting countries in the Middle East and Russia. These imbalances in the current account are often seen as the consequence of the relative inflexibility of the currency regimes in China and some other emerging economies. Thus, global macroeconomic imbalances were the major underlying cause of the crisis. These saving-investment imbalances and consequent huge cross-border financial flows put great stress on the financial intermediation process. The global imbalances interacted with the flaws in financial markets and instruments to generate the specific features of the crisis.

10.1.2 Under-pricing of Risks: Another source of the problem was the significant mis-pricing of risks in the financial system. Easy monetary policy in major financial centres, globalisation of liquidity flows, wide-spread use of highly complex structured debt instruments and the inadequacy of banking supervision in coping with financial innovations, contributed to the severity of the crisis. The persistent under-pricing of risks was suspected by several central banks for quite some time, but it was felt by many that these risks were widely dispersed through financial innovation and that they would not pose any serious problems to the banking system. When the sub-prime crisis did occur, however, it triggered a wide contagion affecting many of the large global financial institutions. Banks ceased to trust each other's creditworthiness leading to difficulties in the money markets in the US, Europe and the UK resulting in drying up of liquidity, since each financial institution attempted to shore up its own liquidity to meet its obligations.

The problems of maturity mismatch in the conduits or structured investment vehicles (SIVs) created by the banks for purposes of securitisation manifested themselves in a sudden spurt in demand for liquidity from banks to meet their liquidity support obligations to the SIVs. It is now realised that the relevant banks had leveraged excessively and had not fully recognised the risks, thus warranting large capital infusion.

10.1.3 Loose Monetary Policy of US: In recent years, monetary policy in the US and other advanced economies was eased aggressively. Policy rates in the US reached 1 percent in June 2003 and were held around these levels for an extended period. In the subsequent period, the withdrawal of monetary accommodation was quite gradual. Assessment of the US monetary policy by experts indicates that the actual policy during the period 2002-06, especially during 2002-04, was substantially looser than what a simple rule would have required. There is clearly evidence that there were monetary excesses during the period leading up to the housing boom.

Excessively loose monetary policy boosted consumption and investment in the US and it was made with purposeful and careful consideration by monetary policy makers. As might be expected, with such low nominal and real interest rates, asset prices also recorded strong gains, particularly in housing and real estate, providing further impetus to consumption and investment through wealth effects. Thus, aggregate demand consistently exceeded domestic output in the US and this was mirrored in large and growing current account deficits in the US over the period. The large domestic demand of the US was met by the rest of the world, especially China and other East Asian economies, which provided goods and services at relatively low costs leading to growing surpluses in these countries.

Furthermore, the availability of relatively cheaper goods and services from China and other EMEs also helped to maintain price stability in the US and elsewhere, which might have not been possible otherwise. Thus, measured inflation in the advanced economies remained low, contributing to the persistence of accommodative monetary policy.

10.1.4 Relaxation of Lending Standards: Apart from creating large global imbalances, accommodative monetary policy and the existence of very low interest rates for an extended period encouraged the search for yield, and relaxation of lending standards. Even as financial imbalances were building up, macroeconomic stability was maintained. Relatively stable growth and low inflation were witnessed in the major advanced economies since the early 1990s and the period was dubbed as the Great Moderation. The stable macroeconomic environment encouraged under-pricing of risks. Financial innovations, regulatory arbitrage, lending malpractices, excessive use of the originate and distribute model, securitisation of sub-prime loans and their bundling into AAA tranches on the back of ratings, all combined to result in the observed excessive leverage of financial market entities.

10.1.5 Regulatory Shortcomings: Some of the regulatory shortcomings identified for the present crisis are as under:

1. The regulators recognised some of the underlying vulnerabilities in the financial sector but failed to take effective action, partly because they may have over-

estimated the strength and resilience of the financial system or they assumed that the risks were well-distributed among entities outside the banking system.

2. The limitations in regulatory arrangements, including the capital adequacy framework, contributed to the growth of unregulated exposures, excessive risk-taking and weak liquidity risk management.
3. Weaknesses in the application of accounting standards and the shortcomings associated with the valuation and financial reporting of structured products played a significant role in the current turbulence through pro-cyclical valuations and lack of full disclosure of true risk profile of banks.
4. Supervisors did not adequately address deterioration in risk management standards in the regulated entities, which did not fully reckon the risks associated with new financial instruments, and there were shortcomings in consolidated supervision.

In short, the major causes of current financial/economic turbulence can be summarized as follows:

1. The prolonged benign macroeconomic conditions gave rise to complacency among many market participants and led to an erosion of sound practices, resulting in adoption of poor credit risk appraisal standards.
2. Some of the standard risk management tools and models used by market participants were not equipped to estimate the potential impact of adverse events for structured credit products.
3. Many investors, including institutional ones, with the capacity to undertake their own credit analysis, did not undertake sufficient in-house examination of the risks in the assets underlying structured investments.
4. The role of credit rating agencies in the recent market developments has been dubious.
5. Weaknesses in public disclosures by financial institutions on the type and magnitude of risks associated with their

on- and off-balance sheet exposures.

6. Excessive risk-taking by the financial institutions/banks in investments based on less than objective assessment of the underlying instruments by rating agencies.
7. Faulty risk management practices in financial markets.
8. Leveraging beyond prudent capital adequacy norms.
9. Inconsistent macroeconomic policies giving rise to domestic and international imbalances.
10. Deficient regulatory and supervisory framework.

10.2 Severity and Impact of the Crisis

The world economy experienced a synchronized downturn extending to the emerging markets with steeper fall in output and trade than earlier anticipated. Global economic activity continues to contract with the advanced economies experiencing their sharpest declines in the post-Second World War period, notwithstanding policy efforts. The financial sector de-leveraging—in conjunction with weak credit markets, falling production and rapidly shrinking global trade—led to a situation of a more prolonged recession. The impact was visible not only in the financial markets but also in the real economy across the globe. Significant fall in various asset prices, the end of a housing construction boom in a number of countries and fall in consumer and business sentiments weighed on economic activity. While all major advanced economies including the US, Euro Area, Japan and the UK witnessed recessionary conditions, the growth in developing countries showed significant moderation. Many economists predicted that the 2008-09 recession would be the worst global recession since the 1930s.

In its publication *World Economic Outlook* (October 2008), the IMF placed the estimated world output growth at 3.9 percent in 2008 which represented a significant slide from a level of about 5.0 percent in 2006 and 2007. By early November, the IMF had revised its forecast for global growth downwards—from 3.9 percent to 3.7 percent for 2008, and from 3.0 percent to 2.2 percent for 2009. Clearly, 2009 proved to be a more challenging year than 2008.

The recent developments suggest that impact is likely to be more protracted and deeper than envisaged by the IMF. In an increasingly globalised economic milieu, these external developments have a major impact on world economy, including the emerging market economies and developing countries through both direct and indirect transmission channels.

Several countries, notably US, UK, Euro Area and Japan are all officially in recession. Confidence in global credit markets continues to be low, and credit lines remain clogged. The tight and hesitant conditions in the credit markets are precipitating erosion of demand which, in turn, is feeding a recession–deflation vicious cycle. Central banks around the world are responding to the developments by aggressive and unconventional injection of liquidity, monetary easing and relaxation of collateral norms and eligibility criteria for their lending to financial institutions.

10.2.1 Impact on Global Capital Market: For the global capital market, developments in the US financial markets have been very critical. The freezing of US money markets has affected normal, routine trade credits and supplier's credit, which is very seldom affected in normal cyclical downturns. Indeed it is one of the reasons that make the current crisis unprecedented. These are likely to be reversed when markets unfreeze. Further, equity disinvestment and repatriation has reduced availability of risk capital for corporate sector worldwide. Still further, medium to long-term flows are likely to be lower as long as the de-leveraging process goes on in the US. A major concern is that the slowdown in OECD countries is turning into a recession with growth estimates for US, EU and Japan being revised downwards virtually every month since September 2008. This will have a negative effect on imports of these countries and consequently on exports of emerging economies.

The present indications are that the turmoil has pushed in a phase of reduced private debt and equity flows to developing countries. International credit and bond markets have shrunk in size, the US money markets have frozen and the cross-border capital flows have moderated. The turmoil has also curtailed cross-border bank lending to developing countries.

10.2.2 Impact on US Dollar: The US dollar generally appreciated against most of the currencies as the US investors were liquidating their positions in overseas equity and bond markets and repatriating the money back to the US. In spite of the deepening of the financial crisis and weakness in economic activity in the US, the flight to safety considerations helped strengthen the US dollar. During 2008-09, the US dollar appreciated against most major currencies including the euro and the pound sterling. The US dollar, however, depreciated against the Japanese yen, as a result of unwinding of carry trades. Amongst Asian currencies also, thc US dollar appreciated against Korean Won, Thai Bhat, Malaysian Ringgit, Indonesian Rupiah and Indian Rupee but depreciated against Chinese Yuan.

10.2.3 Impact on Equity Markets: The year 2008-09 was a dismal year for the stock markets. As a reflection of the economic and financial market outlook, the year was characterized by depressed equity valuations. Consequently, price/earnings ratios in most markets across the world followed a downward trend.

Though the decline in equity valuations was broad-based across all sectors, financial institutions, particularly in Japan, were the worst sufferers. The volatility in the markets was compounded by the lack of detailed information about government rescue packages. The equity markets saw a slight recovery in most countries/regions since mid-March 2009, helped further by the US government announcing the details of the public-private investment programme aimed at repairing balance sheets of financial institutions.

10.3 World Level Remedial Measures

As credit markets froze, central banks across the world, along with the respective governments, responded with both conventional and unconventional measures. To stabilize financial markets and revive credit and capital flows, a number of measures were undertaken by countries across the world. Being epicentre of the crisis, US Government took the lead by sanctioning US$ 700 billion under the Troubled Assets Relief Programme to strengthen the US financial market. Besides injecting a substantial amount of liquidity into the system, policy interest rates were cut by almost all countries. Major central banks decided to ease monetary conditions as inflationary pressures appeared to have receded consequent on decline in international energy and commodity prices.

Given the nature of the crisis, purely national responses have been supplemented by global efforts. At their April 2009 meeting, the G-20 leaders collectively committed to take decisive, coordinated and comprehensive actions to revive growth, restore stability of the financial system, restart the impaired credit markets and rebuild confidence in financial markets and institutions. The crisis has forced macroeconomic policy around the world into clearly uncharted territory. Governments and central banks have taken unprecedented fiscal and monetary policy measures to prevent the global recession from turning into a protracted depression.

10.3.1 Bailout Packages: As the market mayhem manifested in terms of crisis of confidence, resulting in drying up of liquidity, governments and central banks stepped in to restore confidence and assure relief to the beleaguered institutions. Alarmed by the financial catastrophe, governments worldwide led by US, announced bailout packages to control the landslide.

To stabilize financial markets and revive credit and capital flows, a number of measures were undertaken by countries across the world. For example, the US Government sanctioned US$ 700 billion under the Troubled Assets Relief Programme to strengthen the US financial market. Besides injecting a substantial amount of liquidity into the system, policy interest rates were cut by almost all countries. Major central banks decided to ease monetary conditions as inflationary pressures appeared to have receded consequent on decline in international energy and commodity prices.

As the epicentre of the global financial crisis was the US, Fed rate was reduced in stages to 1 percent while European Central Bank cut the short-term rate twice to reach the rate of 3 percent. The Reserve Bank of India too undertook a slew of measures to address the issue of both rupee liquidity and forex liquidity. These included, *inter alia*, reduction in CRR in phases from 9.0 percent to 5.5 percent, lowering the Repo rate from 9.0 percent to 6.5 percent, cutting the SLR by one percentage point to 24 percent, enhancing interest rate ceilings on Non-resident (External) Accounts [NR(E)A] and Foreign Currency Non-resident Accounts [FCNR(A)] deposits, relaxing norms for external commercial borrowings (ECBs) and opening a foreign currency swap window for banks.

Central banks in major industrialised economies, by and large, responded with injection of liquidity for a longer period than is usually done. They also resorted to dilution in the quality of collateral required for liquidity support. Most of these operations have not been conducted at the penal rates expected in such situations. This is an unprecedented package which, some observers believe, is indicative of the seriousness of the underlying problems. In addition, there were some specific institution-oriented operations, namely in US, Germany and the UK. While there have been inflationary pressures in most economies, the US has been faced with a threat of serious slowdown in growth warranting a series of cuts in policy rates in recent times.

10.3.2 G-20 Decisions, April 2009: Meeting of the G-20 [1] member countries held on April 2, 2009 in London, decided to undertake a concerted fiscal expansion amounting to US$ 5 trillion to resolve the global crises. They further agreed for over US$ 1 trillion of additional resources for the world economy through international financial institutions and trade finance. It was agreed to treble resources available to the IMF (US$ 750 billion), to support a new SDRs [2] allocation (US$ 250 billion), to support additional lending by the Multilateral Development Banks (at least US$ 100 billion), to ensure support for trade finance (US$ 250 billion), and to use the additional resources from agreed IMF gold sales for concessional finance for the poorest countries.

The G-20 countries additionally pledged to put in place credible exit strategies to ensure long-term fiscal sustainability and price stability. The following major initiatives were agreed upon:

1. Even-handed and independent IMF surveillance of member economies and financial sectors, of the impact of policies on others, and of risks facing the global economy.
2. To establish the much greater consistency and systematic co-operation between countries, and the framework of internationally agreed high standards.
3. Establishment of a new Financial Stability Board (FSB) with a strengthened mandate, as a successor to the Financial Stability Forum (FSF), including all G-20 countries, FSF members, Spain, and the European Commission. The FSB should collaborate with the IMF to provide early warning of macroeconomic and financial risks and the actions needed.
4. Extension of regulation and oversight to all the important financial institutions, instruments and markets including, for the first time, important hedge funds.
5. FSB and the IMF to monitor progress, working with the Financial Action Taskforce and other relevant bodies, and to provide a report to the next meeting of the G-20 Finance Ministers in Scotland in November 2009.
6. IMF to implement the package of quota and voice reforms agreed in April 2008 and complete the next review of quotas by January 2011. For World Bank also, similar

reform should be completed on an accelerated timescale, to be agreed by the 2010 Spring Meetings.

7. The G-20 members committed to refrain from raising new barriers to investment or to trade in goods and services, imposing new export restrictions, or implementing WTO inconsistent measures to stimulate exports.
8. The G-20 members should not retreat into financial protectionism, particularly measures that constrain worldwide capital flows, especially to developing countries.

The global economic crisis started impacting India from the beginning of 2008. Rising crude prices, along with the global food grain shortage, caused a spill over into the real economy. As inflation rose, India was forced to repeatedly tighten credit and money supply.

By the middle of September 2008, it became apparent that the global credit crisis had deepened and kcy financial institutions were in need of help. Governments and central banks across the world, including India, started intervening to cut interest rates, inject liquidity and recapitalize weakening banks and financial institutions. The scale of intervention—through the various bailouts and other fiscal and monetary measures—has been unparalleled in the history of the global financial system.

10.4 Impact of the Crisis on India

The Indian economy, which was on a robust growth path up to 2007-08, averaging at 8.9 percent during the period 2003-04 to 2007-08, witnessed moderation in 2008-09, with the deceleration turning out to be somewhat sharper than anticipated. While the growth deceleration was primarily driven by the knock-on effects of the global economic crisis, it also reflected to some extent the slowdown associated with cyclical factors. Industrial growth experienced a significant downturn and the loss of growth momentum was evident in all categories, viz. capital, intermediate and consumer goods. A hitherto key growth driver, services sector, witnessed some moderation, notwithstanding a counter-cyclical rise in the growth of community, social and personal services on the back of implementation of the recommendations of Sixth Central Pay Commission.

The adverse conditions for access to external capital, and the depressing effects of the global crisis on domestic business confidence contributed to the moderation in investment demand. The deceleration in private consumption expenditure was partly offset by a sharp increase in Government consumption expenditure emanating from the discretionary fiscal stimulus measures and committed expenditures. The key deficit indicators of the Central Government, viz. fiscal deficit and the revenue deficit as per the revised estimates for 2008-09 were, therefore, significantly higher than the budgeted level as well as those of the preceding year. Implementing the fiscal stimulus packages required the Government to defer the attainment of the stipulated deficit targets under the Fiscal Responsibility and Budget Management (FRBM) Act, 2003.

Corporate performance remained subdued during 2008-09, with the impact on profitability being particularly adverse when growth in sales decelerated. External demand conditions weakened, particularly since October 2008, with the decline in exports resulting in a sharp widening of the merchandise trade deficit.

Large net outflows under portfolio investment and large repayments under short-term trade credit, along with a wider current account deficit led to a decline in reserves. However, India's external debt, debt sustainability indicators and the level of foreign exchange reserves continue to remain at comfortable levels to ensure external stability.

Monetary growth witnessed moderation during 2008-09, reflecting deceleration in bank credit on the back of the slowdown in economic activity emanating from the deepening of the international financial turmoil. RBI, therefore, undertook a number of measures such as cuts in the cash reserve ratio (CRR), unwinding of balances held by the Government with the Reserve Bank under Market Stabilisation Scheme (MSS), open market operations (OMOs) and other measures to ensure ample rupee liquidity in the system.

The impact of world recession could be seen in the moderation of growth rate of the Indian economy in 2008-09 which at 7.1 percent still, however, made India the second fastest growing economy in the World.

In view of the changed environment due to capital outflows and risk aversion, there was a substantial shrinking of non-bank sources of funding in India—such as domestic capital markets, funding from NBFCs and mutual funds and external funding in the form of commercial borrowings and ADRs/GDRs. Accordingly, there was a sudden rush for bank credit from the various sectors of the economy and there were perceptions of credit crunch.

10.5 Remedial Measures Taken by the Government

To counter the negative fallout of the global slowdown on the economy, Indian Government took prompt action by providing substantial fiscal stimulus.

The measures taken by Government to counter the effects of the global meltdown have resulted in a shortfall in revenues and substantial increases in government expenditures during 2008-09 and 2009-2010, leading to a temporary deviation from the fiscal consolidation path mandated under the Fiscal Responsibility and Budget Management (FRBM) Act. In the Final Budget presented to the Parliament on July 6, 2009, the revenue deficit and fiscal deficit for 2008-09 and 2009-2010 were, as a result, higher than the targets set under the FRBM Act and Rules. It means the fiscal policy for the year 2009-10 will continue to be guided by the objectives of keeping the economy on the higher growth trajectory amidst global slowdown by creating demand through increased public expenditure in identified areas.

10.5.1 Policy Response by RBI: RBI has been pro-actively managing liquidity since mid-September 2008 to assuage the liquidity pressures through a variety of measures. The cash reserve ratio (CRR) was reduced from 9 percent (September 2008) to 5 percent by early January 2009 injecting nearly ₹ 1,60,000 crore of primary liquidity in the system. Fresh issuances under MSS were stopped and buyback of existing MSS securities was also resorted to inject liquidity into the system. Following the amendment to the Memorandum of Agreement on the MSS, ₹ 12,000 crore was transferred to the Government cash account from the MSS cash account. Other measures taken by RBI in response to the global financial crisis included cut in the statutory liquidity ratio (SLR), opening of new refinancing windows, refinance to SIDBI and EXIM Banks, and clawing back of prudential norms in regard to provisioning and risk weights.

The existing set of monetary instruments has, thus, provided adequate flexibility to manage the evolving situation. In view of this flexibility, unlike central banks in major advanced economies, RBI did not have to invent new instruments or to dilute the collateral requirements to inject liquidity.

The relative stability in domestic financial markets, despite extreme turmoil in the global financial markets, is reflective of prudent practices, strengthened reserves and the strong growth performance in recent years in an environment of flexibility in the conduct of policies.

Active liquidity management is a key element of the current monetary policy stance. Liquidity modulation through a flexible use of a combination of instruments has, to a significant extent, cushioned the impact of the international financial turbulence on domestic financial markets by absorbing excessive market pressures and ensuring orderly conditions.

The equity markets, which had remained subdued throughout 2008-09, began to pick-up in the last week of

March, in line with the international developments.

Inflation as measured by year-on-year variation in the wholesale price index (WPI), declined from its intra-year peak of 12.9 percent recorded on August 2, 2008 to 0.3 percent as on March 28, 2009 and was reported at 0.12 percent as on September 5, 2009.

In short, the Indian economy has experienced some loss of growth momentum with major drivers of growth witnessing moderation. In particular, the broad-based industrial slowdown, dampened services sector growth, deceleration in private consumption and investment demand along with declining export demand are some of the major concerns facing the Indian economy in the wake of the global recession at the present juncture. The fiscal stimulus packages of the Government and the monetary easing of RBI are expected to arrest the moderation in growth and revive consumption and investment demand in the near future.

10.5.2 Assessment of Policy Response: RBI's policy response was aimed at containing the contagion from the outside—to keep the domestic money and credit markets functioning normally and ensure that the liquidity stress did not trigger solvency cascades. In particular, three objectives were targeted:

1. To maintain a comfortable rupee liquidity position.
2. To augment foreign exchange liquidity.
3. To maintain a policy framework that would keep credit delivery on track so as to arrest the moderation in growth.

This marked a reversal of RBI's policy stance from monetary tightening in response to heightened inflationary pressures of the previous period to monetary easing in response to easing inflationary pressures and moderation in growth in the current cycle. Measures by RBI to meet the above objectives came in several policy packages starting mid-September 2008, on occasion in response to unanticipated global developments, and at other times in anticipation of the impact of potential global developments on the Indian markets.

Policy packages of RBI included, like in the case of other central banks, both conventional and unconventional measures. On the conventional side, it reduced the policy interest rates aggressively and rapidly, reduced the quantum of bank reserves impounded by the central bank and expanded and liberalized the refinance facilities for export credit. Measures aimed at managing forex liquidity included an upward adjustment of the interest rate ceiling on the foreign currency deposits by non-resident Indians, substantially relaxing the external commercial borrowings (ECBs) regime for corporates, and allowing non-banking financial companies and housing finance companies access to foreign borrowing.

The important among the many unconventional measures taken by RBI were the following: (a) a rupee-dollar swap facility for Indian banks to give them comfort in managing their short-term foreign funding requirements, (b) an exclusive refinance window as also a special purpose vehicle for supporting non-banking financial companies, and (c) expanding the lendable resources available to apex finance institutions for refinancing credit extended to small industries, housing and exports.

Reflecting the rapid turn of events that could impair assets down the line, RBI reversed the counter-cyclical regulatory measures introduced in 2006. Taken together, the measures put in place since mid-September 2008 have ensured that the Indian financial markets continue to function in an orderly manner. Taking the signal from the policy rate cut, many of the big banks have reduced their benchmark prime lending rates.

In evaluating the response to the crisis, it is important to remember that although the origins of the crisis are common around the world, the crisis has impacted different economies differently. Importantly, in advanced economies, where it originated, the crisis spread from the financial sector to the real sector. In emerging economies, the transmission of external shocks to domestic vulnerabilities has typically been from the real sector to the financial sector.

Countries have accordingly responded to the crisis depending on their specific country circumstances. Thus, even as policy responses across countries are broadly similar, their precise design, quantum, sequencing and timing have varied. In particular, while policy responses in advanced economies have had to contend with both the unfolding financial crisis and deepening recession, in India, the response has been predominantly driven by the need to arrest moderation in economic growth.

To conclude, India, with its strong internal drivers for growth, has escaped the worst consequences of the global financial crisis. Indian banks had very limited exposure to the US mortgage market, directly or through derivatives, and to the failed and stressed financial institutions.

Recent developments in the World economy have brought forward several new realities that pose severe challenges to macro-economic management, in particular to monetary and regulatory policies globally. Concerns relating to the US slowdown and its intensity have mounted in view of the potential spill over on to the global economy. Threats to the global economy are emanating from advanced economies in sharp contrast to earlier crises which stemmed from the emerging world. Similarly, there are indications that protectionist tendencies have increased around the world in anticipation of the growing possibilities of slower growth in advanced economies.

Still further, linkages between financial sector developments and the real sector have become more worrisome than before, with apprehensions that financial turmoil may spill over to the real sector with adverse implications for employment and growth. With tightening in lending standards, deterioration in asset quality and deceleration in consumer loan demand, there are indications that events in the financial markets are beginning to have a persisting impact on the real economy as well.

Developing countries are exhibiting resilience until now in the face of the global financial turmoil reflecting relatively stronger macroeconomic framework and sustainable macroeconomic balances. However, until how long and to what extent it will persist is uncertain.

In spite of the severity and multiplicity of the adverse shocks, India's financial markets have shown admirable resilience. This is in large part because India's banking system remains sound, healthy, well capitalized and prudently regulated. India’s comfortable foreign exchange reserves position provides confidence to overseas investors.

Since a large majority of Indians do not participate in equity and asset markets, the negative impact of the wealth loss effect that is plaguing the advanced economies should be quite muted. Consequently, consumption demand should hold up well. The farm loan waiver package implemented by the Government should further insulate the agriculture sector from the crisis.

Over the years, India has built an extensive network of social safety-net programmes, including the flagship rural employment guarantee programme. These uniquely Indian versions of automatic stabilizers should protect the poor from the extreme impact of the global crisis.

End Notes

1. The Group of Twenty (G-20) Finance Ministers and Central Bank Governors was established in 1999 to bring together systemically important industrialized and developing economies to discuss key issues in the global economy. The inaugural meeting of the G-20 took place in Berlin, on December 1516, 1999, hosted by German and Canadian finance ministers. The G-20 is made up of the finance ministers and central bank governors of 19 countries: Argentina, Australia, Brazil, Canada, China, France, Germany, India, Indonesia, Italy, Japan, Mexico, Russia, Saudi Arabia, South Africa, South Korea, Turkey, United Kingdom, United States of America. The European Union is the 20th member of the G-20.
2. Special Drawing Rights (SDRs) were created as a new and

additional form of international reserves/liquidity in 1970 under the International Monetary Fund (IMF). Under this scheme, countries receive SDRs as per their share in reserve assets and have an automatic right to draw them from IMF over and above other drawing facilities. SDRs constitute a permanent net addition to international liquidity.

Glossary of Capital Market Terms

Glossary of Capital Market Terms

-A-

Accreting: A description applicable to a range of instruments, e.g. caps, swaps, collars and swaptions, where the notional amount on which the instrument is based increases successively during its life.

Accrued Interest: The interest accruing on a security since the previous coupon date. If a security is sold between two payment dates, the buyer usually compensates the seller for the interest accrued, either within the price or as a separate payment.

Acid Test Ratio: The value of cash equivalents and accounts receivable (the quick assets) divided by current liabilities. Also known as quick asset ratio or liquidity ratio, it is a measurement of corporate liquidity.

Active Portfolio Strategy: A strategy that uses available information and forecasting techniques to seek a better performance than a portfolio that is simply diversified broadly.

Adjusted Beta: The estimation of a security's future beta, which is derived from historical date, but is modified assuming that the security's real beta has tendency to move towards the market average of one.

Agency Orders: Orders that a broker dealer executes for the account of a customer with another professional or retail investor.

Allotment Advice: A letter sent to the successful applicant by the company stating allotment of shares or debentures or other securities against his application. The advice is not negotiable in the market.

Allotment Letter: Document of title issued to investors by companies stating allotment of shares/debentures/other securities to applicants subscribing for such securities or in pursuance of certain contracts entered into in that behalf. These letters are negotiable in the market.

Analyst: A firm/company/an individual who is engaged either on his own behalf or on behalf of any other firm or organization that is regularly publishing securities recommendations based on research either through print media and/or electronic media.

Appreciation: A rise in the price of a security or in the value of one currency in terms of another.

Approved Intermediary: A person duly registered by the SEBI Board under the Securities Lending Scheme, 1997 through whom the lender of securities will deposit the securities and the borrower will borrow the securities.

Arbitrage: Technically, arbitrage consists of purchasing a commodity or security in one market for immediate sale in another market (deterministic arbitrage).

Arbitration: An alternative dispute resolution mechanism provided by a stock exchange for resolving disputes between the trading members and their clients in respect of trades done on the exchange.

Asset-backed Securities: Securities backed by assets that are not mortgage loans. Examples include assets backed by automobile loans, credit card receivables and others.

Asset Management Company: A company which handles the day to day operations and investment decisions of a unit trust.

Auditor: A person who is professionally qualified to examine and scrutinize accounts. He/she inspects records and reports on the profitability and financial position of the company.

Authorized Capital: The amount of capital that a company has been authorized to raise by way of equity and preference shares, as mentioned in the Articles of Association or Memorandum of Association of the company.

Automatic Reinvestment: A fund service giving unit holders/ shareholders the option to purchase additional units/shares using dividend and capital gain distributions.

Average Annual Growth Rate: The average increase in the value of a portfolio over the period of a year.

Averaging: The process of gradually buying more and more securities in a declining market (or selling in a rising market) in order to level out the purchase (or sale) price.

-B-

Badla: Carrying forward of transactions from one settlement period to another without effective delivery. This is permitted only in specified securities and is done at the making up price which is usually the closing price of the last day of settlement.

Bail out of Issue: When the public issue do not get good response from the public or fails to garner minimum subscription, the issuer or promoters approaches the financiers or some persons to arrange subscription to bail out the issue for consideration of buy-back shares subsequent from the financiers at higher price or compensating the financier by payment of interest on the amount of the subscription money paid in the public issue.

Balance Sheet: An accounting statement of a company's

assets and liabilities, provided for the benefit of shareholders and regulators. It gives a snapshot, at a specific point of time, of the assets that the company holds and how the assets have been financed.

Balanced Fund: Funds which aim to provide both growth and regular income as such schemes invest both in equities and fixed income securities in the proportion indicated in their offer documents.

Bancassurance: The phenomenon whereby a financial institution combines the selling of banking products and insurance products through the same distribution channel. Popular in the early 1990s bancassurance rested on the premise that it is easy to cross-sell banking and insurance services because customers feel confident buying insurance from the same institution where they keep their savings.

Banker to an Issue: A scheduled bank carrying on all or any of the issue related activities namely acceptance of application and application monies; acceptance of allotment or call monies; refund of application monies; and payment of dividend or interest warrants.

Bear: A pessimist market operator who expects the market price of shares to decline. The term also refers to the one who has sold shares which he does not possess, in the hope of buying them back at a lower price, when the market price of the shares come down in the near future.

Bear Market: A weak or falling market characterized by the dominance of sellers.

Bench Mark: Security used as the basis for interest rate calculations and for pricing other securities. Also denotes the most heavily traded and liquid security of a particular class.

Bid: An offer of a price to buy as in an auction. Business on the Stock Exchange is done through bids. Bid also refers to the price one is willing to pay for a security.

Bid Spread: The difference between the stated and/or displayed price at which a market maker is willing to sell a security and the price at which he is willing to buy it.

Block Trading: Buying and selling a block of securities usually takes place when restructuring or liquidating a large portfolio.

Blue Chip: The best rated shares with the highest status as investment based on return, yield, safety, marketability and liquidity.

Bond: A negotiable certificate evidencing indebtedness a debt security or IOU, issued by a company, municipality or government agency. A bond investor lends money to the issuer and, in exchange, the issuer promises to repay the loan amount on a specified maturity date. The issuer usually pays the bondholder periodic interest payments over the life of the loan.

Book Building Process: A process undertaken by which a demand for the securities proposed to be issued by a corporate body is elicited and built up and the price for such securities is assessed for the determination of the quantum of such securities to be issued by means of a notice, circular, advertisement, document or information memoranda or offer document.

Book Closure: The periodic closure of the Register of Members and Transfer Books of the company, to take a record of the shareholders to determine their entitlement to dividends or to bonus or right shares or any other rights pertaining to shares.

Book Value: The net amount shown in the books or in the accounts for any asset, liability or owners' equity item. In the case of a fixed asset, it is equal to the cost or revalued amount of the asset less accumulated depreciation (also called carrying value). The book value of a firm is its total net assets, i.e. the excess of total assets over total liabilities.

Boom: A condition of the market denoting increased activity with rising prices and higher volume of business resulting from greater demand of securities. It is a state where enlarged business, both investment and speculative, has been taking place for a sufficiently reasonable period of time.

Break Even Point: The stock price (or price) at which a particular strategy of transaction neither makes nor loses money. In options, the result is at the expiration date in the strategy. A dynamic break-even point changes as time passes.

Broker: A member of a Stock Exchange who acts as an agent for clients and buys and sells shares on their behalf in the market. Though strictly a stock broker is an agent, yet for the performance of his part of the contract both in the market and with the client, he is deemed as a principal, a peculiar position of dual responsibility.

Brokerage: Commission payable to the stockbroker for arranging sale or purchase of securities. Scale of brokerage is officially fixed by the Stock Exchange. Brokerage scales fixed in India are the maximum chargeable commission.

Bubble: A speculative sharp rise in share prices which like the bubble is expected to suddenly burst.

Bull: A market player who believes prices will rise and would, therefore, purchase a financial instrument with a view to selling it at a higher price (opposite of a bear).

Bull Market: A rising market with abundance of buyers and relatively few sellers.

Buoyancy: A rising trend in prices.

Business Day: A day on which the Stock Exchange is open for business and trading in securities.

Buy Back: Repurchase by a company of its own stock or bonds.

-C-

Call Money: The unpaid instalment of the share capital of a company, which a shareholder is called upon to pay.

Call Option: An agreement that gives an investor the right, but not the obligation, to buy an instrument at a known price by a specified date. For this privilege, the investor pays a premium, usually a fraction of the price of the underlying security.

Capital Gain Distribution: Profits distributed to unit holders/shareholders resulting from the sale of securities held in the fund's portfolio for more than one year.

Cash Market: A market for sale of security against immediate delivery, as opposed to the futures market.

Certificate of Deposit: A negotiable certificate issued by a bank, usually for a period of one month to a year, as evidence of an interest bearing time deposit. This may also be offered at a discount.

Circuit Breaker: A system to curb excessive speculation in the stock market, applied by the stock exchange authorities, when the index spurts or plunges by more than a specified per cent. Trading is then suspended for some time to let the market cool down.

Clearing House: A department of an exchange or a separate legal entity that provides a range of services related to the clearance and settlement of trades and the management of risks associated with the resulting contracts. A clearing house is often central counterparty to all trades, that is, the buyer to every seller and the seller to every buyer.

Clearing Member: A member of a clearing corporation or clearing house of the derivatives exchange or derivatives segment of an exchange, who may clear and settle transactions in securities.

Closing Price: The rate at which the last transaction in a security is struck before the close of the trading hours.

Commercial Paper: A short term promise to repay a fixed amount that is placed on the market either directly or through a specialized intermediary. It is usually issued by companies with a high credit standing in form of a promissory note redeemable at par to the holder on maturity and therefore does not require any guarantee.

Common Stock: Units of ownership of a public corporation. Holders of common stock typically have voting rights and receive dividends, but there is no guarantee of dividend payment.

Competitive Bid: An offer made by a person other than the acquirer who has made the first public announcement.

Composite Issues: An issue of securities by a listed company on a public-cum rights basis offered through a single offer document wherein the allotment for both public and rights component of the issue is proposed to be made simultaneously.

Compulsory Delisting: Permanent removal of securities of a listed company from a stock exchange as a penalizing measure at the behest of the stock exchange for not making submissions/complying with various requirements set out in the Listing agreement within the time frames prescribed.

Convergence: Narrowing of the difference between the futures contract and the value of the underlying asset during the final days of the contract.

Conversion Price: The price at which a convertible instrument is converted into shares of the company.

Conversion Ratio: The number of shares which may be acquired upon the conversion of a convertible instrument. The ratio is calculated as instrument's principal amount divided by conversion price.

Convertible Bond: A bond giving the investor the option to convert the bond into equity at a fixed conversion price or as per a pre-determined pricing formula.

Coupon: The interest paid on a bond expressed as a percentage of the face value. If a bond carries a fixed coupon, the interest is paid on an annual or semi-annual basis. The term also describes the detachable certificate entitling the bearer to payment of the interest.

Credit Rating: Credit ratings measure a borrower's creditworthiness and provide an international framework for comparing the credit quality of issuers and rated debt securities. Rating agencies allocate three kinds of ratings: issuer credit ratings, long-term debt, and short-term debt. Issuer credit ratings are amongst the most widely watched. They measure the creditworthiness of the borrower including its capacity and willingness to meet financial needs. The top credit rating issued by the main agencies–Standard & Poor's,

Moody's and Fitch IBCA—is AAA or Aaa. This is reserved for a few sovereign and corporate issuers. Ratings are divided into two broad groups: investment grade and speculative (junk) grade.

Credit Rating Agency: Credit rating agency means a body corporate which is engaged in, or proposes to be engaged in, the business of rating of securities offered by way of public or rights issue.

Credit Risk: The risk that a counterparty will not settle an obligation for full value, either when due or at any time thereafter. Credit risk includes pre-settlement risk (replacement cost risk) and settlement risk (principal risk).

Current Asset: Cash or an item of value expected to be converted into cash within one year or one operating cycle, whichever is longer.

Current Liability: Accounting term for money payable within the current accounting year, on account of trade creditors, taxation, dividends, etc. To these are often added provisions, i.e. any charges or liabilities (various government duties, disputed claims, etc.) which the company may have to settle within the accounting year.

-D-

Daily Margin: The amount that has to be deposited at the Stock Exchange on a daily basis for the purchase or sale of a security. This amount is decided by the stock exchange.

Dalal Street: Street on which The Stock Exchange, Mumbai is situated. Used synonymously for The Stock Exchange, Mumbai.

Dealer: A firm that enters into transactions as a counterparty on both sides of the market in one or more products.

Debentures: Bonds issued by a company bearing a fixed rate of interest usually payable half yearly on specific dates and principal amount repayable on a particular date on redemption of the debentures.

Delisting of Securities: Permanent removal of securities of a listed company from a stock exchange. As a consequence of delisting, the securities of that company would no longer be traded at that stock exchange.

Delivery: Presentation of securities with transfer deeds in fulfilment of a transaction.

Delivery Price: The price fixed by the Stock Exchange at which deliveries on futures are invoiced. Also the price at which the future contract is settled when deliveries are made.

Dematerialise: The process of transforming securities holdings in physical form to those in electronic form through a Depository Participant.

Depository: A system of organisation, which keeps records of securities, deposited by its depositors. The records may be physical or simply electronic records.

Depository Participant (DP): An agent of the depository through which it interfaces with the investor. A DP can offer depository services only after it gets proper registration from SEBI.

Depreciation: A fall in value of a security or security index or a currency in terms of others or its purchasing power.

Depth of Market: The number of shares of a security that can be bought or sold at the best bid or offer price.

Derivative Market: Markets such as futures and option markets that are developed to satisfy specific needs arising in traditional markets. These markets provide the same basic functions as forward markets, but trading usually takes place on standardized contracts.

Derivative: (i) A security derived from a debt instrument, share, loan whether secured or unsecured, risk instrument or contract for differences or any other form of security; (ii) A contract which derives its value from the prices, or index or prices, of underlying securities.

Direct Quotation: The quotation of variable units of domestic currency in terms of fixed units of foreign currency.

Dirty Price: A price for a bond which includes the amount of interest that has accrued on the bond since the date of the last interest payment.

Disclosure: Full and material information given by a company that may allow an investor to take an informed investment decision.

Discount: When a security is quoted at a price below its nominal or face value, it is said to be at a discount.

Dividend: Payment made to shareholders, usually once or twice a year out of a company's profit after tax. Dividend payments do not distribute the entire net profit of a company, a part or substantial part of which is held back as reserves for the company's expansion. Dividend is declared on the face value or par value of a share, and not on its market price.

Dumping: In the securities market the offering of large amounts of stock without regard for the effect on prices on the market. In the international trade, the selling of goods overseas below cost to get rid of a surplus or to gain a competitive edge over the foreign firms.

-E-

Electronic Fund Transfer (EFT): System which utilizes computer and electronic components in order to transfer money or financial assets. EFT is information based and intangible.

Employee Stock Option: "Employee stock option" means the option given to the whole-time directors, officers or employees of a company which gives such directors, officers or employees, the benefit or right to purchase or subscribe at a future date, the securities offered by the company at a predetermined price.

Entry Fee: Fee paid by an investor when purchasing units in a trust or managed fund. The fee is included in the price that new investors pay.

Equity: The ownership interest in a company of holders of its common and preferred stock.

Equity Premium: The difference between the expected return from holding stock and from holding riskless bonds.

Equity Trust: Unit Trust which invests mainly in equity shares with a component in cash and in fixed interest investment.

Ex: Means 'Without'. A price so quoted excludes recently declared dividends (xd) rights (xr) or bonus shares (xb).

Exchange: Regulated market place where capital market products are bought and sold through intermediaries.

Exchange Rate Risk: The risk that adverse movements in exchange rates lead to capital losses in assets or revaluation of liabilities.

Exchange-traded Derivative: A derivative which is listed and traded at an organised market-place. Derivatives exchanges generally provide standardised contracts and central clearing facilities for participants.

Exchange Traded Funds (ETF): A security that tracks an index but has the flexibility of trading like a stock.

Ex-Dividend Date: The date on or after which the buyer of a security is not entitled to the dividend already declared.

Ex-Right Date: The date on which the official quotation for a share is marked XR i.e. ex rights, in the daily official list.

-F-

Face Value: The value that appears on the face of the scrip, same as nominal or par value of share/debentures.

Firewall: A barrier designed to prevent losses or risks taken in one part of a financial institution from weakening other parts of institution.

Floating Stock: The fraction of the paid up equity capital of a company which normally participates in day to day trading.

Floor: Trading hall of the Stock Exchange where transactions in securities take place. The trading ring where members and their assistants assemble with their order books for executing the order of their constituents.

Floor Price: The minimum offer price below which bids cannot be entered. The issuer company in consultation with the lead book runner fixes the floor price.

Flow Back: Securities recently placed in the markets that are resold on the issuers' national market. It is one of the major risks in an equity placement because it may frustrate the objective of internationalization of the equity market and cause downward pressure on its market price.

Foreign Institutional Investor: An institution established or incorporated outside India which proposes to make investment in India in securities; provided that a domestic asset management company or domestic portfolio manager who manages funds raised or collected or brought from outside India for investment in India on behalf of a sub-account, shall be deemed to be a foreign institutional investor.

Forward Contract: An agreement for the future delivery of the underlying commodity or security at a specified price at the end of a designated period of time. Unlike a future contract, a forward contract is traded over the counter and its terms are negotiated individually. There is no clearing house for forward contracts, and the secondary market may be non-existent or thin.

Forward Rate Agreement: A forward contract on interest rates in which the rate to be paid or received on a specific obligation for a set period of time, beginning at some time in the future, is determined at contract initiation.

Futures Contract: An exchange traded contract generally calling for delivery of a specified amount of a particular financial instrument at a fixed date in the future. Contracts are highly standardized and traders need only agree on the price and number of contracts traded.

-G-

Gilt Edged: A term used to describe a bond, generally issued by the Government or issued with a Government Guarantee so much so that there are no doubts about the ability of the issuer to pay regular interest and the principal amount to the bond holders.

Global Depository Receipts: Any instrument in the form of a depository receipt or certificate (by whatever name it is called) created by the Overseas Depository Bank outside India and issued to non-resident investors against the issue of ordinary shares or foreign currency convertible bonds of issuing company.

Good Delivery: Proper delivery by a seller to the buyer of the securities without any defect so that they can be transferred without any additional documentation.

Goodwill: The part of value of a business that is based on good customer relations, high employee morale and other factors.

Growth Fund: Unit trusts or mutual funds which invest with the objective of achieving mostly capital growth rather than income. Growth funds are mostly more volatile than conservative income or money market funds because managers invest on shares or property that are subject to larger price movements.

Guaranteed Coupon: Bonds issued by a subsidiary corporation and guaranteed as to principal and/or interest by the parent corporation.

-H-

Hand Delivery: Delivery and payment on the date stipulated by the stock exchange.

Hedge: An asset, liability or financial commitment that protects against adverse changes in the value of or cash flows from another investment or liability. An unhedged investment or liability is called an "exposure". A perfectly matched hedge will gain in value what the underlying exposure loses or lose what the underlying exposure gains.

Hedge Funds: Private investment pools that invest aggressively in all types of markets, with managers of the fund receiving a percentage of the investment profits. The name is something of a misnomer since a hedge fund's raison d'etre is quite the opposite of hedging.

Hedge Ratio: The proportion of one asset required to hedge against movements in the price of another.

Hot Issue: A security that is expected to trade in the after market at a premium over the public offering price.

Hot Money: Short-term international capital movements, motivated by interest rate differential or revaluation hopes/devaluation fears.

Hypothecation: Pledging assets against a loan. The ownership of the asset or the income from the asset is not transferred, except that in default of repayment of loan the asset may be sold to realize its value. Brokers will accept shares as collateral for loans to finance purchase of shares or to cover short sales.

-I-

Indexed Asset: An indexed asset has coupon and principal payments that are adjusted upward in response to increase in price level. This adjustment is intended to compensate lenders for the decline in purchasing power of loan repayments.

Indian Depository Receipt: A receipt, evidencing an underlying foreign security, issued in India by a foreign company which has entered into an agreement with the issuer and depository, custodian and depository or underwriters and depository, in accordance with the terms of prospectus or letter of offer, as may be prescribed.

Initial Public Offering (IPO): The first public issue by a public limited company.

Insider: Any person who, is or was connected with the company or is deemed to have been connected with the company, and who is reasonably expected to have access, connection, to unpublished price sensitive information in respect of securities of a company, or who has received or has had access to such unpublished price sensitive information.

Insider Trading: Practice of corporate agents buying or selling their corporation's securities without disclosing to the public significant information which is known to them but which has not yet affected the price.

Interim Dividend: A dividend payment made during the course of a company's financial year. Interim dividend, unlike the final dividend, does not have to be agreed in a general meeting.

Investment Banker: Financial conglomerate which conducts a full range of investment related activities from advising clients on securities issues, acquisitions and disposal of businesses, arranging and underwriting new securities, distributing the securities etc.

Investment Company: A corporation, trust or partnership that invests pooled unit holder/shareholder money in securities appropriate to the organization's objective. Mutual funds, close–ended funds and unit investment trusts are the three types of investment companies.

Investment Profit: Profit which results from the difference between the purchase and selling prices of a security. Trading profit is short term while investment profit is medium or long term.

Issuer: An entity which is in the process of issuing its securities (also known as the "originator").

-J-

Jobber: Member brokers of a stock exchange who specialize, by giving two way quotations, in buying and selling of securities from and to fellow members. Jobbers do not have any direct contact with the public but they serve the useful function of imparting liquidity to the market.

Jobbers Spread: The difference between the price at which a jobber is prepared to sell and the price at which he is prepared to buy. A large difference reflects an imbalance between supply and demand.

-K-

Kapli: A standard form used by the broker to inform the stock exchange of his transactions for the purpose of matching a settlement.

Killer Bees: Law firms, proxy solicitors and public relations firm employed to help a company management fight off an unfriendly takeover.

Kiss Principle: Advice given by old pros to neophyte brokers on how they should explain to investors such sophisticated investment concepts as options and arbitrage.

-L-

Lagging Indicators: Market indicators showing the general direction of the economy and confirming or denying the trend implied by the leading indicators or concurrent indicators.

Lame Duck: A defaulter on a stock exchange who is not able to meet his market commitment and financial obligations of his business.

Law of One Price: An economic rule stating that a given security must have the same price regardless of the means by which one goes about creating that security. This implies that if the payoff of a security can be synthetically created by a package of other securities, the price of the package and the price of the security whose payoff it replicates must be equal.

Lay Off: The sell off by an issuer of any or all unsubscribed shares in a rights offering to the underwriters at the subscription price.

Leading Indicators: Market indicators that signal the state of the economy for the coming months.

Lead Manager: The merchant banker(s) associated with the issue and responsible for due diligence and other associated issue related activities.

Legal Risk: The risk of loss because a law or regulation is applied in an unexpected way or because a contract cannot be enforced.

Letter of Offer: A letter of offer is a document addressed to the shareholders of the target company containing disclosures of the acquirer/Persons Acting in Concert (PACs), target company, their financials, justification of the offer price, the offer price, number of shares to be acquired from the public, purpose of acquisition, future plans of acquirer etc.

Liquid Assets: Proportion of listed unit trust's or mutual fund portfolio that is kept in cash or easily encashable assets to meet any request for redemption.

Liquidity Risk: The risk that a solvent institution is temporarily unable to meet its monetary obligations.

Listed Company: A company which has any of its securities offered through an offer document listed on a recognized stock exchange and also includes public sector undertakings whose securities are listed on a recognised stock exchange.

Listing: Formal admission of a security into a public trading system.

-M-

Maintenance Margin: The minimum margin that must be maintained on a futures contract.

Manipulation of Financial Markets: Activities whose objective is to alter prices in financial markets through the use of techniques that result in unnatural market prices, often through the use of wash sales or reporting of fictional or apparent market prices.

Margin: An advance payment of a portion of the value of a stock transaction. The amount of credit a broker or lender extends to a customer for stock purchase.

Markdown: A charge levied by a broker when buying securities on its own account from a customer. (These purchases as principals from customer take place at the best bid prices minus a commission equivalent to markdown).

Market Maker: A member firm who give two way quotation for particular security(ies) and who is under an obligation to buy and sell them subject to certain conditions such as overall exposure, spread etc.

Market Model: This relationship is sometimes called the single-index model. The market model says that the return on a security depends on the return on the market portfolio and the extent of the security's responsiveness as measured by beta (b). In addition, the return will also depend on conditions that are unique to the firm. Graphically, the market model can be depicted as a line fitted to a plot of asset returns against returns on the market portfolio.

Market Price: The last reported sale price for an exchange traded security.

Marking Up Prices: Prices fixed by the stock exchange to facilitate settlement of bargains in the specified securities, particularly at the end of the settlement period.

Mark-up: A charge levied by a broker when selling securities from its own account to a customer. These sales as principals to a customer take place at the best ask price plus a commission equivalent to mark-up.

Maturity Value: The amount an investor receives when a security is redeemed at maturity not including any periodic interest payments. The value usually equals the par value although on zero coupon, compound interest and multiplier bonds, the principal amount of the security at issuance plus the accumulated investment return on the security is included.

Merchant Banker: Any person who is engaged in the business of issue management either by making arrangement regarding selling, buying or subscribing to securities or acting as manager, consultant, adviser or rendering corporate advisory service in relation to such issue management.

Money Laundering: Process of converting the proceeds of illegal activities–disclosure of which would trigger financial losses or criminal prosecution–into real or financial assets whose origins remain effectively hidden from law enforcement officials and from society in general.

Money Market: The market encompassing the trading and issuance of short-term non-equity debt instruments, including treasury bills, commercial paper, bankers' acceptance, certificates of deposits etc. The market may be local or international.

Money Market Mutual Funds: Schemes investing exclusively in safer short-term instruments such as treasury bills, certificates of deposit, commercial paper and inter-bank call money, government securities, etc.

Mortgage-backed Securities: Securities backed by mortgage loans, including pass-through securities, modified pass-through securities, mortgage-backed bonds, and mortgage pay-through securities.

Mortgage Trust: Unit trust which invests in mortgage loans. Effectively the unit trust invests money in real estate and receives an interest return with security over the property which has been purchased. The interest which is charged on mortgage trust loans is normally higher than that other sources of finance like banks so that the investor usually receives a very competitive rate or return.

Moral Hazard: The risk that a party to a transaction has not entered into a contract in good faith has provided misleading information about its assets, liabilities or credit capacity or has an incentive to take unusual risks in a desperate attempt to avoid losses.

Mutual Funds /Unit Trusts: Mutual fund is a mechanism for pooling the resources by issuing units to the investors and investing funds in securities in accordance with objectives as disclosed in offer document. A fund established in the form of a trust to raise monies through the sale of units to the public or a section of the public under one or more schemes for investing in securities, including money market instruments.

-N-

NASDAQ: Acronym for the National Association of Security Dealers Automated Quotations. This is an organization that does exactly what its name stands for. The system provides a computerized information network through which brokers, banks and other investment professionals can obtain up to the minute price quotations on securities traded over the counter.

Negotiated Dealing System (NDS): Electronic platform for facilitating dealing in Government securities and money market instruments, introduced by RBI.

Net Dividend: Dividend after deduction of tax payable from gross dividend.

Net Liquid Assets: Cash and readily marketable securities minus current liabilities of a company. This is the strictest test of a company's ability to meet current debt obligations.

Net Working Capital: The excess of current assets over current liabilities.

Net Worth: The aggregate value of the paid up equity capital and free reserves (excluding reserves created out of revaluation), reduced by the aggregate value of accumulated losses and deferred expenditure not written off, including miscellaneous expenses not written of.

New Issue: Shares of a company offered to the public, through a public issue, for the first time to be listed on the Stock Exchange.

Net Asset Value (NAV): The current market worth of a mutual fund's share. A fund's net asset value is calculated by taking the fund's total assets, securities, cash and any accrued earnings, deducting liabilities, and dividing the remainder by the number of units outstanding.

Non-deliverable Swap: Similar to a non deliverable forward, the only difference being that settlement for both parties is done through a major currency.

-O-

Off Balance Sheet Risk: Risk relative to operations that are not reflected in variation of the institutions assets or liabilities, when undertaken, but are reflected when profit or loss occurs.

Offer Document: As per SEBI DIP guidelines, offer document means prospectus in case of a public issue or offer for sale and letter of offer in case of a rights issue.

Offer Period: The period between the date of entering into memorandum of understanding or the public announcement, as the case may be and the date of completion of offer formalities relating to the offer.

Offer Price: Price at which units in trust can be bought. It often includes an entry fee. It also refers to the price at which securities are offered to the public.

Ombudsman: An independent person appointed to hear and act upon citizen's complaint about government services. Invented in Sweden, the idea has been widely adopted. For example, groups of banks, mortgage lenders and insurance companies in various countries have appointed ombudsmen to attend to the complaints of their customers. Customers who use the ombudsman's (free) service retain their full right to take legal action should they not agree with the ombudsman's decision.

Open-ended Scheme: An open-ended fund or scheme is one that is available for subscription and repurchase on a continuous basis.

Open Market Operation: Purchase or sale of government securities by the monetary authorities (RBI in India) to increase or decrease the domestic money supply.

Open Order: An order to buy and sell a security that remains in effect until it is either cancelled by the customer or executed.

Opening Price: The rate at which the first transaction in a security is struck after the opening of the market.

Operating Income: Net sales less cost of sales, selling expenses, administrative expenses and depreciation. The pre-tax income from normal operations.

Operational Risk: The risk that deficiencies in information systems or internal controls could result in unexpected losses.

Order Book: It is an 'electronic book' that shows the demand for the shares of the company at various prices.

OTC (Over the Counter): A financial transaction that is not made on an organised exchange. Generally, the parties must negotiate all the details of each transaction or agree to use simplifying market conventions.

Overtrading: A broker/dealer overpays a customer for a security to enable the customer to subscribe to another security offered by that broker/dealer at a higher mark-up than the loss to be sustained when the firm sells the customer's first security at prevailing market prices.

-P-

Paid in Capital: The difference between par or book-keeping, value of a security and the amount realized from the sale or distribution of those shares by the company.

Paid up Capital: The amount of capital, both equity and preference, paid up by the shareholders against the capital subscribed to by them.

Par Value: Means the face value of securities.

Pari Passu: A term used to describe new issue of securities which have same rights as similar issues already in existence.

Partial Tender Offer: A tender offer for less than all target shares; specifies a maximum number of shares to be accepted, but does not announce bidder's plans with respect to the remaining shares.

Participating Preference Shares: The right of certain preference shareholders to participate in profits after a specified fixed dividend contracted for is paid. Participation right is linked with the quantum of dividend paid on the equity shares over and above a particular specified level.

Pink Sheets: Listing of over the counter stocks, the dealers who trade them and the prices at which these dealers are willing to buy and sell. Printed daily on loud pink newsprint and found in brokerage house and many banks.

Players: A diverse range of intermediaries and institutional investors active in the capital market. This includes securities firms, broker dealers, commercial banks, merchant banks, unit trust/mutual fund etc.

Pooling: The basic concept behind mutual funds in which a fund aggregates the assets of investors who share common financial goals. A fund uses the investment pool to buy a diversified portfolio of investments and each mutual fund share purchased represents ownership in all the funds underlying securities.

Portfolio: A collection of securities owned by an individual or an institution (such as a mutual fund) that may include stocks, bonds and money market securities.

Preferential Allotment: Further issue of shares/securities convertible into equity shares at a later date, to a select group of persons in preference to all the existing shareholders of the company.

Premium: If an investor buys a security for a price above its eventual value at maturity he has paid a premium for it.

Profit Taking: Realizing profits by closing out an existing position.

Prospectus: Any document described or issued as a prospectus and includes any notice, circular, advertisement or other document inviting deposits from the public or inviting offers from the public for the subscription or purchase of any shares in, or debentures of, a body corporate.

Proxy: One who votes for and on behalf of a shareholder at a company meeting.

Public Issue: An invitation by a company to public to subscribe to the securities offered through a prospectus.

Put Option: An option that gives the right to sell a fixed number of securities at a specified price (the strike price) within a specified period of time.

-Q-

Quotation: The NASDAQ requirement that a market maker who receives order from another broker dealer executes the order at its displayed price on NASDAQ for the normal unit of trading or its displayed size, whichever is greater.

-R-

Real Time Gross Settlement (RTGS): Concept designed to achieve sound risk management in the settlement of inter-bank payments. Transactions are settled across accounts held at the Central Bank on a continuous gross basis where settlement is immediate, final and irrevocable.

Record Date: A date on which the records of a company are closed for the purpose of determining the stockholders to whom dividends, proxies rights etc. are to be sent.

Registrar to an Issue: The person appointed by a body corporate or any person or group of persons to carry on the activities of collecting applications from investors in respect of an issue; keeping a proper record of applications and monies received from investors or paid to the seller of the securities and assisting body corporate or person or group of persons in-determining the basis of allotment of securities in consultation with the stock exchange; finalising of the list of persons entitled to allotment of securities; processing and despatching allotment letters, refund orders or certificates and other related documents in respect of the issue.

Rematerialisation: The process of converting electronic holdings into physical securities through a Depository Participant.

Reverse Book Building: Reverse book building is similar to the process of book building, which is aimed at securing the optimum price for a company's share. In reverse book building the investors' aim is to sell the shares to exit the company.

Rigged Market: Manipulation of share price to attract buyers and sellers to the riggers advantage.

Rights Issue/Rights Shares: The issue of new securities to existing shareholders in a fixed ratio to those already held.

Rolling Settlement: The practice on many stock markets of settling a transaction a fixed number of days after the trade is agreed.

Ruling Price: The current market price of a security.

Run: A run involves a person creating activity in a security by successively buying or selling that security. The intention is that the increased activity would, in case where the person is buying, attract others to buy and push up the price. At that point, those organizing the run would then attempt to sell out at a financial gain. This is sometimes known as "pumping and dumping."

-S-

Screen-based Trading: Form of trading that uses modern telecommunication and computer technology to combine information transmission with trading in financial markets.

Secondary Market: The market for previously issued securities or financial instruments.

Securitization: The process of homogenizing and packaging financial instruments into a new fungible one. Acquisition, classification, collateralization, composition, pooling and distribution are functions within this process.

Selling Short: A manner in which an investor sells securities he does not posses in the hope of buying them back later at a lower price.

Sensitive Index: A share price index based on 30 active scrips developed by the Bombay Stock Exchange with 1978-79 as the base year.

Share Transfer Agent: Any person, who on behalf of any body corporate maintains the record of holders of securities issued by such body corporate and deals with all matters connected with the transfer and redemption of its securities. It can also be a department or division (by whatever name called) of a body corporate performing the above activities if, at any time the total number of the holders of securities issued exceed one lakh.

Short Covering: Buying of stocks by a seller to complete his previous commitments.

Short Position: In futures, the short has sold the commodity or security for future delivery; in options, the short has sold the call or the put and is obligated to take a futures position if he or she is assigned for exercise.

Stakeholder: Any individual or group who has an interest in a firm; in addition to shareholders and bondholders, includes labour, consumers, suppliers, the local community and so on.

Stamp Duty: The ad valorem duty payable by buyer for transfer of shares in his name. Also payable on contracts issued by a stock broker.

Standard Price: The standard price of a security is generally worked out as a weighted average price of all recorded transactions for that security adjusted to the nearest rupee.

Stock Dividend: A dividend paid to stockholders in shares of stock of the issuing corporation, issued to stockholders or record out of the unissued stock of the corporation, involving no payment of cash, and used to reflect positive interest in the security.

Stock Exchange: Any body of individuals, whether incorporated or not, constituted for the purpose of assisting, regulating or controlling the business of buying, selling or dealing in securities.

Stock Option: The right to purchase shares of common stock in accordance with an agreement, upon payment of a specified amount; a compensation scheme under which executives are granted options to purchase common stock over an extended option period at a stated price.

Swap Reversal: An Interest rate swap designed to end counterparty's role in another Interest rate swap, accomplished by counterbalancing the original swap in maturity, reference rate, and notional amount.

Sweat Equity: A sweat equity share is an equity share issued by the company to employees or directors at a discount or for consideration other than cash for providing know-how or making available rights in the nature of intellectual property rights or value additions.

Systemic Risk: Risk that affects an entire financial market or system, and not just specific participants. It is not possible to avoid systemic risk through diversification.

-T-

Takeover Panel: An acquirer who proposes to acquire shares through a mode which is not specifically covered under takeover regulations may seek exemption from the applicability of the provisions of the offer process by making an application. SEBI has constituted a panel consisting of independent persons to examine such applications which is called the Takeover Panel.

Target Company: A target company is a listed company i.e. whose shares are listed on any stock exchange and whose shares or voting rights are acquired/ being acquired or whose control is taken over/being taken over by an acquirer.

Technical Position: Condition of the market created by various internal factors and opposed to external forces.

Tender Offer: Tender offer means an offer by a company to buy back its specified securities through a letter of offer from the holders of the specified securities of the company.

Thin Markets: Characterized by relatively few transactions per unit of time and where price fluctuations are high relative to the volume of trade.

Tracking Error: When using an indexing or any other benchmarking strategy, the amount by which the performance of the portfolio differed from that of the benchmark.

Trading Member: A member of the derivatives exchange or derivatives segment of a stock exchange who settles the trade in the clearing corporation or clearing house through a clearing member.

Transfer Agents: An agent designated by the company to carry out the function of transfer of shares.

Transferee: The buyer of the securities in whose favour the securities are bought to be registered is known as the Transferee.

Transferor: The seller of the security is the transferor of the security.

-U-

Underwriter: One who does underwriting. A financial organization that handles sales of new securities which a company or municipality wishes to sell in order to raise money. Typically the underwriters will guarantee subscription to securities say, an issue of equity from the company at a stated price, and are under an obligation to purchase securities up to the amount they have underwritten, should the public not subscribe for the issue.

Underwriting: An agreement with or without conditions to subscribe to the securities of a body corporate when the existing shareholders of such body corporate or the public do not subscribe to the securities offered to them.

-V-

Value at Risk (VAR): VAR is the maximum loss over a target horizon such that there is a low, pre-specified probability that the actual loss will be larger.

Vanilla Issue: A straight fixed rate issue which has terms and conditions usually accepted as being conventional to a particular securities market.

Vanishing Companies: Companies which have not complied with specific provisions of the listing agreement and regulations of the stock exchanges, and are not physically traceable at the registered address mentioned in the offer document.

Venture Capital: Professional moneys co-invested with the entrepreneur usually to fund an early stage, more risky venture. Offsetting the high risk is the promise of higher return that the investor takes. A venture capitalist not only brings in moneys as "equity capital" (i.e. without security/charge on assets) but also brings on to the table extremely valuable domain knowledge, business contacts, brand equity, strategic advice, etc. He is a fixed interval investor, whom the entrepreneurs approach without the risk of "takeover".

Vertical Spread: Buying and selling puts or calls of the same expiration month but with different strike prices.

Vesting: The process by which the employee is given the right to apply for shares of the company against the option granted to him in pursuance of employee stock option scheme.

Volatility: Volatility equates to the variability of returns from an investment. It is an acceptable substitute for risk; the greater the volatility, the greater is the risk that an investment will not turn out as hoped because its market price happens to be on the downswing of a bounce at the time that it needs to be cashed in. The problem is that future volatility is hard to predict and measures of past volatility can, themselves, be variable, depending on how frequently returns are measured (weekly or monthly, for example) and for how long. Therefore, putting expectations of future volatility into predictive models is of limited use, but resorting to using past levels of volatility is equally limited.

Volume of Trading: The total number of shares which changes hands in a particular company's securities. This information is useful in explaining and interpreting fluctuation in share prices.

Voluntary Delisting: Delisting of securities of a body corporate voluntarily by a promoter or an acquirer or any other person other than the stock exchange.

-W-

Warrant: An options contract often sold with another security. For instance, corporate bonds may be sold with warrants to buy common stock of that corporation. Warrants are generally detachable.

Window Dressing: A manoeuvre often engaged in by companies, banks, mutual funds etc., at the end of the accounting period in order to impress stock holders who will be receiving the report showing that funds are better managed and invested than what might have been drawn up.

Wolf: Speculators who make a kill in the market.

Writer: A person who issues an option. The individual who at the end of the day has to buy or sell the asset on which the option is written, should the person who holds the option wish to exercise his rights.

-X-

X Dividend: A term meaning 'without dividend'. A stock bought on or after the X- dividend day will not pay the purchaser the dividend already declared.

-Y-

Yankee Bond: A bond offering in the US domestic market by a non-U.S. entity registered with the SEC.

Yield to Maturity (YTM): The rate of return anticipated on a bond if it is held until the maturity date. YTM is considered a long term bond yield expressed as an annual rate.

Yuppie Scam: The name given to Wall Street insider trading scandal after a host of smart young lawyers, bankers and arbitrageurs were found to be in the dealing ring.

-Z-

Zero Coupon Bond: A bond that pays no interest while the investor holds it. It is sold originally at a substantial discount from its eventual maturity value, paying the investor its full face value when it comes due, with the difference between what he paid initially and what he finally collected representing the interest he would have received over the years it was held.

Zero Coupon Yield Curve: A yield curve of zero coupon bonds. Market practice is often to derive this curve theoretically from the par yield curve. Frequently used to derive discount factors. Also known as spot yield curve.

Bibliography

Bibliography

Alexander, S.S., 1961, "Price Movements in Speculative Markets: Trends or Random Walks", *Industrial Management Review* II, May, 7-26.

Alexander, S.S., 1964, "Price Movements in Speculative Markets: Trends or Random Walks, Number 2", *Industrial Management Review* V, Spring, 25-46.

Alford, A, "The Effect of the Set of Comparable Firms on the Accuracy of the Price-earnings Valuation Method," *Journal of Accounting Research 30*, (1992), pp. 94-108.

Ariel, R.A., 1987, "A Monthly Effect in Stock Returns", *Journal of Financial Economics*, 18, 161-174.

Asquith, P., 1983, "Merger bids, Uncertainty and Stockholder Returns", *Journal of Financial Economics,* 11, 51-83.

Asquith, P., and Mullins, David W., 1983, "The Impact of Initiating Dividend Payments on Shareholders' Wealth", *Journal of Business* 56, 77-96.

Asquith, P., and Mullins, David W., 1986, "Equity Issues and Offering Dilution", *Journal of Financial Economics* 15, 61-89.

Baker, M. and Ruback, R., "Estimating Industry Multiples," *working paper*, Harvard University, Cambridge, MA., 1999.

Ball, R. and Brown, P., "An Empirical Evaluation of Accounting Income Numbers", *Journal of Accounting Research*, 1968, pp.159-178.

Barua, S.K. and Raghunathan, V., 1986, "Inefficiency of the Indian Capital Market", *Vikalpa*, Vol. 11, No. 3, 225-229.

Barua, S. K., Raghunathan, V and Varma, J.R., 1994, "Research on the Indian Capital Market: A Review", *Vikalpa*, January-March, Vol. 19, No. 1, 15-27.

Basu, S., "Investment Performance of Common Stocks in Relation to their Price-Earnings Ratios: A Test of Efficient Market Hypothesis", *Journal of Finance,* Vol. 32, 1977, 663-682.

Beatty, R.P., Riffe, S.M., and Thompson, R., "The Method of Comparables and Tax Court Valuations of Private Firms: An Empirical Investigation," *Accounting Horizons 13*, (1999), 177-199.

Beaver, W., Clarke, R., and Wright, W., "Association between

Unsystematic Security Returns and Magnitude of Earnings Forecast Errors", *Journal of Accounting Research*, 1979.

Beaver, W., Lambert, R., and Morse, D., "The Information Content of Security Prices", *Journal of Accounting and Economics*, 1980, 3-28.

Beaver, W., Lambert, R., and Ryan, S., "The Information Content of Security Prices: A Second Outlook", *Journal of Accounting and Economics 9*, 1987, 139-57.

Biswal, Pratap Chandra and Kamaiah, B., 2001, "Stock Market Development in India: Is there any Trend Break?", *Economic and Political Weekly*, January 27, 377-2001.

Blanchard, Oliver J. and Watson, Mark, "Bubbles, Rational Expectations and Financial Markets", *NBER Working Paper*, No. 945, 639-660.

Boatsman, J. and Bakin, E., "Asset Valuation with Incomplete Markets," *The Accounting Review 56*, 1981, 38-53.

Bombay Stock Exchange, *www.bseindia.com.*

Broca Dilbagh S., 1994, "Volatility Shifts in Stock Market Returns: A Look at Emerging Markets", *Vikalpa*, January-March, Vol. 19, No. 1, 47-53.

Broca, Dilbagh S., 1995, "Monitoring Volatility Changes on the Bombay Bourse: A Control Chart Approach", *Vikalpa*, July-September, Vol. 20, No. 3, 43-51.

Brown, P., Kleidon, A.W. and Marsh, T.A., 1983, "New Evidences on the Nature of Size Related Anomalies in Stock Prices", *Journal of Financial Economics.*

Byun, Jinho and Rozeff, Michael S., 2003, "Long-run Performance after Stock Splits: 1927 to 1996", *The Journal of Finance*, Vol. LVIII, No. 3, 1063-1085.

Campbell, John Y. and Shiller Robert J., 1988, "Stock Prices, Earnings, and Expected Dividends", *The Journal of Finance,* July, Vol. XLIII, No. 3, 661.

Campbell, John Y., Lo, A. W., and Mackinlay, A. C., 1997, *The Econometrics of Financial Market*, Princeton University Press, Princeton, New Jersey.

Chakrabarti, B.B., 2003, "State of the Equity Market", *Portfolio Organizer,* March, 16-19.

Chan, K.C., Chen, N., and Hsieh, D., 1983, "An Exploratory Investigation of the Firm Size Effect", *Manuscript, University of Chicago*, Cited in Dimsom, 1988.

Charest, Guy, 1978, "Dividend Information, Stock Returns, and Market Efficiency-II", *Journal of Financial Economics* 6, 297-330.

Chaudhuri, S.K., 1991a, "Short-run Share Price Behaviour: New Evidences on Weak Form of Market Efficiency", *Vikalpa*, Vol. 16, No. 4, 17-21.

Chaudhuri, S. K., 1991b, "Seasonality in Share Returns: Preliminary Evidences on Day-of-the-Week Effect", *Chartered Accountant*, November, Vol. 40, No. 4, 407.

Cheng, Pao L. and Deets, M. King, 1970, "Portfolio Returns and the Random Walk Theory", *Journal of Finance,* 11-30.

Cochrane, John H., 1991a, "A Critique of the Application of Unit Root Tests", *Journal of Economic Dynamics and Control*, 15, 275-284.

Collins, D.W., Kothari, S.P., and Rayburn, J.D., "Firm Size and the Information Content of Prices with Respect to Earnings*", "Journal of Accounting and Economics 9*, 1987, 111-38.

Conrad, J. and Kaul, G., 1988, "Time-Variance in Expected Returns", *Journal of Business*, 61(4), 409-425.

Cooke, T.J., and Rozeff, M.S., 1984, "Size and Earnings/Price Ratio Anomalies: One Effect or Two?", *Journal of Financial and Quantitative Analysis*.

Copeland, T., Koller, T., and Murrin, J., "Valuation", New York, Willey, 1994.

Cox, John C. and Stephen, A. Ross, 1976, "The Valuation of Options for Alternative Stochastic Finance," *Journal of Financial Economics* 3, 145-166.

Da, Z. and Schaumburg, E., 2008, "Relative Valuation and Analyst Target Price Forecasts", *Working Paper*, July, accepted at *Journal of Financial Markets*.

Damodaran, Aswath, 1993, "A Simple Measure of Price Adjustment Coefficients", *The Journal of Finance*, March, Vol. XLVIII, No. 1, 387-400.

Damodaran, A., "Damodaran on Valuation", New York, Willey, 1996.

Dann, Larry V., 1981, "Common Stock Repurchases: An Analysis of Returns to Bondholders and Stockholders", *Journal of Financial Economics* 9, 113-138.

DeBondt, Werner F.M. and Thaler, Richard H., 1985, "Does the Stock Market Overreact?" *The Journal of Finance,* July, Vol.

XL, No. 3, 793-805.

Dennis, Patrick J. and Strickland, Deon, 2002, "Who Blinks in Volatile Markets, Individuals or Institutions?", *The Journal of Finance*, October, Vol..LVII, No.5, 1923-1949.

Desai, Hemang, and Jain, Prem C., 1997, "Long-run Common Stock Returns Following Stock Splits and Reverse Splits", *Journal of Business,* Vol. 70, 409-433.

Dhankar, R.S. and Kumar, R., 2007, "Portfolio Performance in relation to Price Earnings Ratio: A test of Efficiency under Different economic conditions", *The Journal of Applied Finance*, Vol. 13, No. 12007, 37-45.

Diba, Behzad T. and Grossman, Herschel I., 1987, "On the Inception of Rational Bubbles", *Quarterly Journal of Economics*, August 697-700.

Fama, E. and French, K., "Value vs Growth: the International Evidence", *Journal of Finance* 53, 1998, 1975-1999.

Feinstone, Lauren J., 1987, "Minute By Minute: Efficiency, Normality, and Randomness in Inta-Daily Asset Prices", *Journal of Applied Econometrics*, Vol. 2, 193-214.

Feltham, G.A., and Ohlson, J.A., 1995, "Valuation and Clean Surplus Accounting for Operating and Financial Activities", *Contemporary Accounting Research 11,* 689-731.

Figlewski, Stephen, 1978, "Market 'Efficiency' in a Market with Heterogeneous Information", *Journal of Political Economy*, Vol. 86, No. 4, 581-597.

Finnerty, Joseph E., 1976 b, "Insiders and Market Efficiency", *The Journal of Finance,* Vol. XXXI, No. 4, September 1976, 1141-1148.

Fisher, Lawrence, 1996, "Some New Stock Market Indexes", *Journal of Business*, 39(2), 191-225.

Flavin, Marjorie, 1983, "Excess Volatility in the Financial Market: A Reassessment of the Empirical Evidence", *Journal of Political Economy,* October, 929-956.

Flood, Robert P. and Hodrick, Robert J., 1986, "Asset Price Volatility, Bubbles and Process Switching", *Journal of Finance*, Vol. 41, 831-842.

Fogler, H. Russell, 1978, *Analyzing the Stock Market: Statistical Evidence and Methodology*, Grid Inc., Columbus, Ohio.

Gaba, Prakash, 2003, "Reasons for Volatility in the Market", *Portfolio Organizer*, February, 51-52.

Gill, S., 2003, "P/E Ratio Revisited", *Finance India*, Vol. XII No. 3, September, 937-951.

Givoly, Dan and Palmon, Dan, 1985, "Insider Trading and the Exploitation of Inside Information: Some Empirical Evidence", *The Journal of Business* 58 (January), 69-87.

Godfrey, Michael D., Granger, Clive W. J. and Morgenstern, Oskar, 1964, "The Random-Walk Hypothesis of Stock Market Behaviour", *Kyklos,* January, Vol. XVII, 1-30.

Gordon, M., "The Investment Financing and Valuation of the Corporation", Homewood, III: Richard D. Irwin, 1962.

Goyal, M.M., 1992, "Security Returns in an Inefficient Market", *Indian Journal of Finance and Research*, July, Vol. 2, No. 2, 61-67.

Gupta, L.C., Jain, P.K., and Gupta, C.P., "Indian Stock Market P/E Ratios: A Scientific Guide to Investors and Policymakers", *Society for Capital Market Research and Development*, 1998, 19-98.

Huang, Y., Tsai, C.H., and Chen, C.R., 2007, "Expected P/E, Residual P/E, and Stock Return Reversal: Time-Varying Fundamentals or Investor Overreaction?" *International Journal of Business and Economics,* Vol. 6, No. 1, 11-28.

Irina, I., Alexander, P., and Ivan, K., "Adjustments to Market Multiples-Based Valuation in Emerging Markets: Empirical Study for Russia", *Working paper,* Corporate Finance Centre, Higher School of Economics, Moscow, Russia, 2007.

Jegadeesh, Narasimhan and Titman, Sheridan, 1993, "Returns to Buying Winners and Selling Losers: Implications for Stock Market Efficiency", *The Journal of Finance*, March, Vol. XLVIII, No. 1, 65-91.

Jensen, Michael C., 1968, "The Performance of Mutual Funds in the Period 1945-1964", *The Journal of Finance*, 389-416.

Johnson, Keith B., 1966, "Stock Splits and Price Change", *The Journal of Finance*, December, Vol. XXI, 675-686.

Kaplan, S.N., and Ruback, R.S., 1995, "The Valuation of Cash Flow Forecasts: An Empirical Analysis," *The Journal of Finance 50,* 1059-1093.

Kim, M. and Ritter, J., 1999, "Valuing IPOs," *Journal of Financial Economics 53*, 409-437.

Kuhn, F.S., 1970, *The Structure of Scientific Revolutions*, The University of Chicago Press. Chicago.

Laeven, Luc, 2003, "Does Financial Liberalisation Reduce Financing Constraints?", *Financial Management,* Spring, Vol. 32, Issue 1, 16-20.

Liu, J., Nissim, D., and Thomas, J., 2002, "Equity Valuation Using Multiples", *Journal of Accounting Research*, Vol. 40 No. 1, March, pp. 135-172.

Liu, J., Nissim, D., and Thomas, J., 2002, "International Equity Valuation using multiples", *Working Paper*, September.

Liu, J., Nissim, D., and Thomas, J., "Is Cash Flow King in Valuations", *Financial Analyst Journal,* Vol. 63, No. 2, CFA Institute, 2007.

Malik, N.S., 2006, "Active Portfolio Management: A Study of Country Funds of Developed and Emerging Markets of the World", (ed.) by O.P. Gupta and others.

Ohlson, J.A., "Earnings, Book Value and Dividends in Equity Valuation", *Contemporary Accounting Research,* 1995, 661-687.

Ou, J.A. and Penman, S.H., 1989, "Accounting Measurement, P/E Ratio and Information Content of Security Prices", *Journal of Accounting Research,* Current Studies on the Information Content of Accounting Earnings, Vol. 27, 111-144.

Palepu, K., Healey, P., and Bernard, V., 2000, "Business Analysis and Valuation", 2nd edition, Cincinnati, Ohio: South Western College Publishing.

Pandey, I.M. and Bhat, Ramesh, 1987, "Efficient Market Hypothesis: Understanding and Accepting in India, *Working Paper No. 691*, July-September, Indian Institute of Management, Ahmedabad.

Penman, S.H., 1997, "Combining Earnings and Book Value in Equity Valuation", *Working Paper,* July.

Penman, S.H., "The Articulation of Price-Earnings Ratios and Market-to-Book Ratios and the Evolution of Growth", *Journal of Accounting Research 34,* Fall 1996a, 253-259.

Poterba, James M. and Summers, Lawrence H., 1988, "Mean Reversion in Stock Prices", *The Journal of Financial Economics*, 22, 27-59.

Reinganum, M.R., 1981 "Misspecification of Capital Asset Pricing: Empirical Anomalies Based on Earnings' Yields and Market Values", *Journal of Financial Economics* 9, March, 19-46.

Reinganum, M.R., 1982 "A Direct Test of Roll's Conjecture on the Firm Size Effect", *Journal of Finance.*

Reserve Bank of India, *www.rbi.org.in.*

Roberts, H., 1959, "Stock-Market Patterns and Financial Analysis: Methodological Suggestions", *Journal of Finance*, 14,1-10.

Roll, R., 1983, "Vas Is Das? The Turn of the Year Effect and the Return Premium of Small Firms", Journal *of Portfolio Management*, 9, 18-28.

Roll, Richard, 1981, "A Possible Explanation of the Small Firm Effect", *Journal of Finance.*

Roll, Richard, 1988, "R^2", *Journal of Finance,* July, Vol. XLII, No. 3, 541-566.

Rosenberg, B. and Rudd, A., 1982, "Factor Related and Specific Returns of Common Stocks: Serial Correlation and Market Efficiency", *Journal of Finance*, May.

Roy, Malay K. and Karmakar, Madhusudan, 1995, "Stock Market Volatility: Root and Results", *Vikalpa,* January-March, Vol. 20, No. 1, 37-48.

Securities Exchange Board of India, *www.sebi.gov.in.*

Sehgal, S. and Tripathy, V., 2005, "Size Effect in Indian Stock Market", *VISION*, MDI Gurgaon, Vol. 9, No. 4, October-December 2005, 27-42.

Seth, A.K., and Gupta, Saloni, 2005, "Understanding Volatility at BSE: A Quality Control Approach (Implications for Investors), *Decision*, Vol. 32, No.1, January-June.

Skogsvik, K. and Skogsvik, S., 2001, "P/E Ratios in Relative Valuation–A Mission Impossible", *Working Paper*, The Economic Research Institute, Stockholm School of Economics, Stockholm, Sweden, April.

Tasker, S.C., 1998, "Industry-Preferred Multiples in Acquisition Valuation", *Working Paper*, Cornell University, Ithaca, NY.,

Vaidynathan, R. and Gali, Kantikumar, 1994, "Efficiency of the Indian Capital Market", *Indian Journal of Finance and Research* Vol. V, No. 2, 27-40.

Vermaelen, Theo, 1981, "Common Stock Repurchases and Market Signalling: An Empirical Study", *Journal of Financial Economics* 9, 139-183.

Wallis, W. and Roberts, H., 1956, *Statistics: A New Approach*, Glencoe, III, Free Press.

West, Kenneth D., 1988, "Bubbles, Fads and Stock Market Volatility Tests: A Partial Evaluation, 1986", *The Journal of Finance*, July, Vol. XLIII, No. 3, 639-660.

Yalawar, Y.B., 1985, "Bombay Stock Exchange: Rate of Return and Efficiency", *Indian Economic Journal*, Vol. 35, No. 4, 68-121.

Index

Index

The capital market has been an important source of funding for larger companies and the opening of the economy to portfolio flows from Foreign Institutional Investors (FIIs). In recent years, it has produced a buoyant capital market where companies have raised significant funds through new issues. However, this mechanism has been used mainly by the larger companies to raise funds. We do not have effective institutions that can channel equity funding to smaller companies and start-ups. In a knowledge economy, we need to do much more to encourage the growth of venture capital funds and angel investors.

Government of India,
Planning Commission,
Twelfth Five Year Plan (2012-17).